SERVING YOU THROUGH THE YEARS............

Book II

A history of more of the business families that have served Stowmarket for generations.

by

Sue Cowling and Steve Williams

A Suffolk Family History Society Publication
2004

This book is dedicated to the people of

Stowmarket

without whose help it could not have been written.

Cover illustration : Daniel Wright.
Title page : Steve Williams

DESIGNED AND TYPESET FOR SFHS BY
Mike Durrant
AUGUST 2004

Published by: Suffolk Family History Society 2004
ISBN 1-905111-00-2
Printed in England by St Edmundsbury Press, September 2004

CONTENTS

ACKNOWLEDGEMENTS

In the preparation of this second book, we have again received invaluable help and encouragement from many friends and colleagues. We would like to thank the Suffolk Family History Society for their sponsorship and the following individuals who provided the information on behalf of the featured families, supplied photographs, various examples of commercial stationery and who granted us permission to reproduce them:

Len **Abery**, Mary **Potter** & Marjorie **Norman** *(Chapter 1)*; Tony **Burrows**, Dennis **Francis** & Poppy **Stewart** *(Chapter 2)*; the late Mary **Cooper**, the late Edna **Cooper**, Ivy **Bailey** & Barry **Cooper** *(Chapter 3)*; Kathleen **Reid**, Raymond **Day** & Elizabeth **Arbon** *(Chapter 4)*; Pamela **Dent**, the late John **Dent**, the late Barbara **Denny**, Jane **Rolfe** & Berice **Jordon** *(Chapter 5)*; Jean **Ince**, Rosemary **Black**, Ron **Kingsley**, John **Kingsley** & Derek **Moore** *(Chapter 6)*; the late Vic **Gordon**, Marjorie and Bernard **Cole** & Jane **Gordon** *(Chapter 7)*; Sheilagh **Maycock**, Christine **White** & Kieron **Palmer** *(Chapter 8)*; Nigel **Mayhew**, Millie **Manning**, Kieron **Palmer** & Rita **Gibbons** *(Chapter 9)*; John **Mosesson**, Rosemary and Jack **Gascoine** & Ken **Read** *(Chapter 10)*; Wray **Nunn**, Vic **Cobbold** & Edna **Weingaertner** *(Chapter 11)*; Pat **Baxter**, Paul **Baxter**, Ella **Boast**, John **Stammers**, Harold **Rush**, Ray **Francis**, John **Wright**, Ian **Button**, Stan **Mayhew**, Roger **Miles**, Jack **Mayhew**, Ray **Bullett** & Len **Savill** *(Chapter 12)*; Olive & Peter **Edwards** *(Chapter 13)*; Beryl **Reed**, Eileen **Black**, Bunty **Wincer**, Jane **Popham**, the late Rev John **Pugh**, Jack **Ray**, Brenda **Jarvis**, Bert **Tyte** & Jill **Wright** *(Chapter 14)*; Jerry **Revett**, Bob **Malster**, Tim **Oxbrow**, Robin **Cowling**, Eddie **Cordle**, Vera **Hearn**, Bill **Calver**, Denny **Reeve**, Barry **Shaw**, Cyril **Horrex** & Brian **Chilvers** *(Chapter 15)*; Michael **Simkin**, the late Don **Flett**, Don **Flett** jnr., Gordon **Graham**, Davidson Martin **Graham**, Joyce **Clover**, Roy **Fidler** & Mary **Potter** *(Chapter 16)*; Paddy **Tibbenham**, Roger **Tombs** & Peter **Jordon** *(Chapter 17)*; John **Williams**, Jean **Williams**, Jennifer **Bridger**, Joy **Ayling-Turner** & the late Hazel **Farrow** *(Chapter 18)*; Gwendolen **Turner**, Rick **Durrant**, the late Ernest **Durrant**, Mary and Cyril **Hall** & Mary **Potter** *(Chapter 19)*; the late Topsy **Webb**, Bob **Webb**, Trevor **Meggs**, the late Jean **George**, Stuart and Christine **Basten** & David **Williams** *(Chapter 20)*; Nic **Portway** & Bob **Malster** *(Chapter 21)*.

We especially thank the following:

Chris **Blanch**, our proof reader;
Ivan **Codd** for his help, and access to his vast historic photographic collection; &
Desmond **Codd**, for producing numerous copies; and their permission to use them;
Mike **Durrant**, for processing all our data & photographs into this book form on his computer;
Daniel **Wright** for designing and producing our front cover.

We also thank:

Geoff **Clarke** (E. A. Film Archive) for processing film we discovered whilst researching this project;
Linden **Clements** for photographic assistance;
John **Humphreys** and **Don Rednall** Stowmarket Group Chairmen S.F.H.S. for their support;
Charles Knight for the use of old advertisements;
Our families - Robin & Wyn **Cowling**, Katherine **Taylor** & Kevin **Girling**;
Harold & Marjorie **Williams**, Kerry **Burn** & Owen **Williams**,
for their support and tolerance during this project;
Suffolk Record Office, Ipswich and Bury St Edmunds branches.
Stowmarket Town Council.

Sue Cowling & Steve Williams

FOREWORD

Derek A Palgrave FFHS

It is indeed a privilege to be invited to contribute a foreword to this second volume, compiled by Sue Cowling and Steve Williams, recording some more families and their commercial activities in Stowmarket. There is no doubt that Volume I was a considerable success both in terms of the way it had captured the interaction between family history and business development in this Suffolk market town and also in terms of the popular interest it engendered amongst the very large number of people who purchased copies.

In a sense, Volume I was very effective publicity for Volume II: those family businesses not included the first time, for one reason or another, came forward with information, anecdotes, photographs and suggestions for coverage of additional businesses, asking if another book was planned. Their enthusiasm soon inspired the authors to commit themselves to a significant expansion of their original project, a challenge that Sue and Steve could relish.

Now, six years on, Volume II is published, featuring twenty-one more businesses with their family connections, including many aspects of food and drink, clothing, services, tools and equipment, building, transport and communications. All are carefully documented and well illustrated. Like its predecessor, this book embodies careful and detailed research by the authors. It is a genuine contribution to our understanding of local business history and as such is another important milestone.

Derek A Palgrave,
Patron, The Suffolk Family History Society

PREFACE

It hardly seems six years ago in 1998 that Steve and I, having eventually collected together the mini family histories of forty-three of the business families of Stowmarket, suddenly realised the enormity of what we had actually collated and put between two hard covers. Even at the launch and subsequent first rush of the selling of *'Serving You Through the Years'* we still had to pinch ourselves to make sure that it was not a dream. But in a way it was, because this book was an achievement, with so much of the living history of the people, who played such a vital role in the growth and development to make Stowmarket a thriving market town in the heart of Suffolk and put its inhabitants in the spotlight.

We promised ourselves a year off, so that we could devote time to our long-suffering families, to catch up with each other and to give our studies a good clean and tidy up. Not a chance, for even whilst the book was being bound in Cornwall, we were already at work on a chapter for Stearn's the chemist in the Market Place, just to 'record the details and hold it on file.' Or so we thought. People were soon stopping us in the street to suggest other families, for which there simply was not room in the first book, so it looked as though our next six years were mapped out for us.

Steve and I are great believers that if it is meant to happen, then it will, so the rallying call went out to our 'team' and a special request to the Suffolk Family History Society to the effect that there *could* possibly be a second volume. The answer came back that if we did the research, then the request would be considered most favourably. This is what we now have: a further twenty-one families where the business has been passed down for more than one generation, making a total of sixty-four families in all. We are totally indebted to our 'team' once more: Ivan Codd, Des Codd, Linden Clements, Geoff Clarke, Dan Wright, Chris Blanch, the Stowmarket Town Council and of course our long-suffering editor and typesetter, Mike Durrant, whose help has been invaluable.

One small recent issue to be considered is the fact that Steve and I married in April this year, posing the question of which surname I should like to see in print. For ease and continuity, therefore, I have decided to write in my maiden name, as a compliment to my parents. At least this clarification will help future generations of family historians!

Once again, we present to the town of Stowmarket our second volume to complement the first - this is your history, of which you may be justifiably proud; Steve and I have just completed another link in the chain of your recorded history.

Sue Cowling
August 2004

It has been six years since *'Serving You Through the Years'* was first published and although we were fairly confident that there would be enough interest to warrant the three thousand books we insisted were printed, we are nevertheless amazed at its success and are still basking in the praise that has been lavished upon us. However, early on we had to acknowledge that, for various reasons, there were some families that were notably absent from that book. The main reason for this was that we did not have a contact name or had been told there was no-one left to give us the family details we needed to follow the format we had been working to. Finally it became a matter of space, so to make it viable we limited the first book to forty-three families.

After S. Y. T. T. Y. was 'up and running' and we began to wonder what we were going to do next, more information started coming through and people began offering up fresh names and contacts; we then decided we could not let these chances of recording the complete picture of Stowmarket's business families slip by. Again we armed ourselves with notepad and pencils as well as a convenient mini tape recorder and began researching a second set of families. We are still often amazed by the amount of coincidences and chance happenings that seem to guide us to be in the right place at the right times to find seemingly lost bits of data that may appear small and insignificant at the time, but like a piece of a jigsaw puzzle, when it is put with all the other facts and figures, it helps to create a bigger and more detailed picture.

I would like to take the opportunity in these few lines to thank all the families who have shown us incredible trust and kindness in the process of researching both of our books on the business families. In the course of the entire project we not only have learnt a lot more about Stowmarket's past, but we have also become experts in tea-tasting. We have been able to unearth many more interesting photographs which add to the wealth of material that the late Harry Double produced. Indeed we are indebted to him for the legacy he left us with his books which we feel has provided the bedrock of interest to enable us to follow in his footsteps.

As the trend for small, family-run businesses is consigned to the history books, not just in Stowmarket, but throughout the country, we feel privileged to have been able to document for future researchers a period when personal service was the norm, the customer was always right and nothing was too much trouble if it helped to secure a sale.

Steve Williams
August 2004

INTRODUCTION

Some six years ago Sue and Steve published their excellent book *'Serving You Through the Years.'* It was extremely well-received by local people and others at home and abroad. With the experience gained from their first publication and considerable further research, Sue and Steve have now produced their second book on the same subject, to add to our knowledge of past traders and businesses in Stowmarket.

We are most grateful to them for their researching of the past and for their promotion of the increasingly popular study of local and family history.

For those of us who have spent most of our lives in Stowmarket, it is a great pleasure to be reminded of how our town used to be, with memories rekindled of childhood days, of visits to the sweetshops and trips to the many and varied food and clothes shops with our parents. No thought was ever given to shopping elsewhere.

In recent years many changes have taken place in our town and our lives in general. However, the past will not be forgotten as long as we have dedicated local historians to record our history and heritage.

Don Rednall
Chairman, Stowmarket Group, Suffolk Family History Society

Abery's/Oliver's

SWEETSHOP & DELICATESSEN

Where the Job Centre now stands in Ipswich Street once stood a shop, remembered by many as **Abery's** sweetshop, which had to be reached by climbing up three steps from the street. The first shop owned by the family was originally 1, Stricklands Road, on the corner of Stricklands Road and Ipswich Street and was started by Arthur **Oliver** and his wife Maude (née **Woollard**) in February 1932, the property being rented from the Catholic Church. The venture started due to Arthur having fallen from his bicycle after skidding on an icy road and breaking his leg. Arthur Oscar **Oliver** was born in Bridge Street, Stowmarket on March 6th 1878, son of John **Oliver**, a Mill Band Maker and Jane **Bridgeman**. Alice Maude (Maude) **Woollard**, daughter of Thomas **Woollard** an engine driver and Elizabeth **Lay**, was born August 28th 1881 at Bramford. The 1881 census shows the family living in Ipswich Street with John **Oliver**, strap maker, aged fifty-five, born Westhorpe with his thirty-two year old wife Jane, born Combs, and their children: Joseph, sixteen, a tanner's labourer, Alice **Bridgeman**, a step-daughter aged thirteen, Percy aged ten, all born Combs, as well as William aged nine, Ada aged six, Arthur aged three and Stanley aged one, all born in Stowmarket. The **Woollard** family was living at 'Parish Pond', Bramford, with Thomas shown as a twenty-two year old engine driver born at Blakenham and Elizabeth, his twenty-three year old wife, born at Bramford.

Arthur married Maude at Claydon Church on December 5th 1914 and had two daughters, Marjorie Irene born January 17th 1916 and Betty Vida born January 1st 1921. During this period Arthur's profession was given as groom/chauffeur. In the Kelly's directory for 1937 their entry reads, **Oliver** Arth. O. confectioner at 1, Stricklands Road. The main core of the business was sweets, cigarettes, tobacco, groceries and some greengrocery as well as their own home-made ice cream, the ice for which came covered with a blanket from the Ipswich Ice Company. Their ice-cream was so popular that it was necessary to make two batches per day, and was described as being 'hard work', as it had to be churned by hand. Marjorie helped in the shop by weighing some of the many variety of sweets, which included 'Blue Bird' toffees at five for a penny, into paper bags. The main range

Oliver's first shop on the corner of Stricklands Road and Ipswich Street previously Kidd's sweetshop

of cigarettes included Woodbines, Player's and Craven 'A'. It was at about this time that Mars Bars were introduced as confectionery and **Oliver's** was the first shop in Stowmarket to stock them, priced at 2d each (1p).

Abery's shop, 51 Ipswich Street

The family worked long hours starting at 6:00 in the morning till 11:00 at night. Then in 1939 they had notice to vacate the premises, so they moved their entire stock overnight to 51, Ipswich Street, which had originally been a private town house known as Ipswich House, owned by Walter **Smith**, a corn merchant, before becoming a 'board residence' under a Mrs **Chapman.** They were able to carry on trading the next day. The Stricklands Road shop was demolished and a bomb shelter was built in preparation for the on-coming war with Germany. The site is now a fenced cycle park.

During the early part of the war, Betty was working at **Juby's** store in Ipswich Street and was witness to the bombing of the Congregational Church on Friday 31st January 1941. Around this time it was popular for many Stowmarket girls to travel to dances held at the Claydon/Barham Workhouse; it was at one such event in 1941 that Betty met Leonard Frank (Len) **Abery** who was serving in the Middlesex Regiment and had been involved with the Dunkirk Evacuation during 1940. After that Len managed to complete a three-year University course in Radar Mechanics, crammed into six months' hard work. He spent the rest of the war based mainly at Harlow repairing radar sets. This involved him covering a large area which included the East Coast from Clacton to Felixstowe. Len had been born July 16th 1918 in Holland Park, London, son of Frederick **Abery**, a high-class builder/ joiner working in the Park Lane and Mayfair districts of London and Louisa (née **Bell**).

Len and Betty married at Stowmarket Parish Church on November 7th 1942. When Len was demobilised in January 1946 he worked in Acton, London for a short while, but as Betty did not like this style of living, when late in 1946 Arthur and Maude announced their imminent retirement, Len and Betty returned to Stowmarket to take over the business, living over the shop. The changeover period took about three weeks and the same line of business was continued. For a few years after the end of the war, although sweets and some groceries were still on ration coupons, Len and Betty built up the business, their policy being to always stock the best and during this time a five pound order was considered to be good business. They were the first in the town to stock **Schweppes**' drinks and ran a special campaign for Ryvita, "buy two and slim twice as fast". Len and Betty also introduced a cheese counter into their shop, importing various French and Dutch varieties which included the blue cheeses such as Gorgonzola,

Len and Betty Abery 1946

Roquefort and Camembert as well as Swiss cheeses like Emmental and Gruyère; they also bought dairy produce such as butter, eggs and clotted cream from local farms. This was soon expanded into quite an exotic delicatessen, stocking such items as calamari (octopus), frogs' legs and snails and introducing new types of food into the diet of local people. London suppliers sent their representatives to the shop, taking orders for such delicacies as Ham, Sausage, Schinkenwurst, Leberwurst, Schinken (uncooked pork) and to complement this Betty roasted her own hams, one per day and these were to be seen hanging up in the shop and sold for 2/6d (12½p) per ¼lb (113g). Hungarian Salami was also a big seller; however Len did decline chocolate-covered ants when his supplier offered them to him! A delivery service was provided and Len's car was used to transport grocery orders to business and farming families within a five/six mile radius of Stowmarket, which included Haughley, Woolpit and Old Newton etc. The shop's tobacco department sold all the normal requisites as well as loose tobacco and snuff. From the end of the war, items that had been on ration and short supply were gradually introduced into the shop; these included **Heinz** Salad Dressing and Tomato Ketchup etc. During this period Len and Betty's daughter, Mary, was born over the Ipswich Street shop on Valentine's Day, February 14th 1952.

The shop consisted of just one room, which was always well stocked, situated on the left of the door as you entered from the street, but in the run-up to Christmas, Len and Betty would vacate their sitting room on the right-hand side of the door. During this period the room was used as an extension to the shop from whence five hundred boxes of chocolates, five hundred tins of biscuits, specialised Christmas puddings and

Another view of the Ipswich Street shop

ground almonds were displayed as well as boxes of specialised Christmas Crackers that Len bought from a supplier in Norwich. They were usually completely sold out in a very short space of time.

As well as his business interests, Len felt that he could serve the community in other ways. He was a founder member of the Stowmarket Chamber of Trade, of which he was President for three years. At that time the Chamber boasted one hundred members. During the 1950's Len was also a member the Stowmarket Urban District Council, being a Councillor for a total of sixteen years. His other interests throughout that whole period included helping out as an electrician for the Stowmarket Dramatic Society and on Sundays, for five years, he was a volunteer driver for the Stowmarket ambulance. He was a member of the Red Cross for fifty years. He also used to enjoy giving lectures to local Women's Institute groups about delicatessens, which enhanced the growing popularity for such enterprise.

In August 1957 Arthur **Oliver** died at Felixstowe, where they had made their home since retiring from the business. His wife Maude died at Ipswich Hospital twelve years later in July 1969.

In the 1960's the Ipswich Street premises, like the first shop, were demolished, the road to the corner of Milton Road was widened and the new Job Centre was built on the site.

Ronnie **Cole** of **Cole's** Furnishers owned the Ipswich Street property and when in 1963 the lease on the shop expired, Len and Betty decided not to renew the lease or look for other premises to continue the business. Instead they moved to a house in Finborough Road and both began working for G. F. **Ray** and Sons' grocery store at 15 - 17 Bury Street, where Len was manager for nine years and Betty served in the shop. When **Ray's** closed at the introduction of decimalisation in 1971, Len took his expertise to the Co-op grocery department, where after a while he became their 'trouble-shooter' by going around to any of their branches as and when needed. He retired in 1979.

Len believes that **Abery's** were forerunners of the modern style of delicatessen/ wholefood mode of shopping and admits to being surprised by his own success in introducing such acquired tastes as snails and frogs' legs to the post-war population of Stowmarket. ❑

Your " MACE " Grocer

L. F. ABERY

51 IPSWICH STREET

STOWMARKET

'Phone 419

VISIT OUR

DELICATESSAN COUNTER

You will find many unusual and exciting Foods

——□——

We Deliver in Your District

Burrows'

FRUITERER & GREENGROCER

The property currently occupied by **Parkyn's Estate Agency** was once a thriving fruit and vegetable business under the ownership of Samuel **Burrows** and family. The first appearance of the Burrows' name in any of the business directories was in a 1900 Kelly's directory which states 'Burrows **Samuel**, fruiterer, Ipswich Street & Bury Street'. A 1904 Rate Book entry has Samuel mentioned at premises in Bury Street and Station Road, but by 1912 the business appears at 6 Market Place, which is the property that they were to become synonymous with for the next seventy years.

Samuel was born at Combs on the 12th February 1877, the fourth child of Samuel **Burrows** and Sarah Ann (née **Grimwood**). The 1881 census shows the family living in Combs as: Samuel aged thirty-six, tanner's labourer, Sarah A., wife, thirty-six, with children Fanny aged twelve, Emily aged seven, Martha aged five, Samuel aged four, Charles W. aged two and eight month old Walter G., the family listed as all being born at Combs. Three more children were added to the family after the census. These were John R. born 1883, Grace E. born 1884 and Arthur born 1886. However, the 1891 census shows Samuel senior as a widower with daughter Fanny as the housekeeper, Emily and Martha both dressmakers, Samuel junior, agricultural labourer, with Charles, Walter, John, Grace and Arthur all scholars.

When Samuel (Sam) **Burrows** junior, aged twenty-two, married Harriet Amelia **Denny**, aged twenty-three, daughter of James **Denny** (miller) and Harriet (née **Baker**) of Stowupland at Stowmarket Congregational Church on the 1st November 1899, his profession was given as fruiterer, which means that by that time he had already begun establishing himself in business selling fruit and vegetables from a small shop in Bury Street, probably where the Red Cross charity shop now is. Interestingly Sam's sister,

Sam and Harriet Burrows outside No 6 Market Place, circa 1908

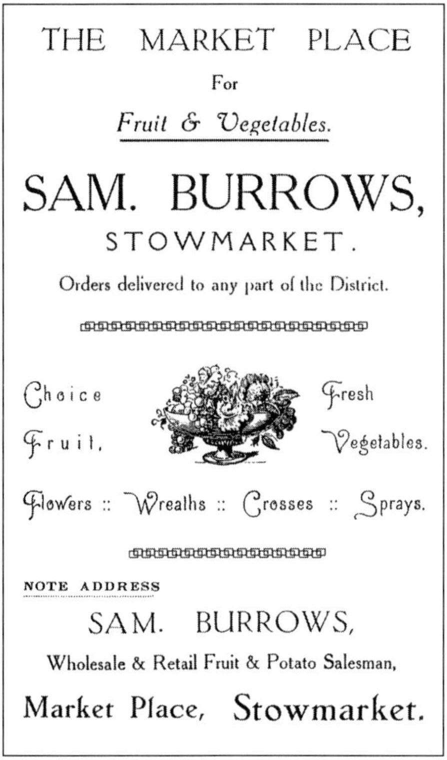

A Burrows' advertisement from a 1931 Shopping Guide

Fanny, married Alfred **Tricker**, a fruiterer of Sudbury, a year later. Sam's family was living in Ipswich Street when the first of their five children, Doris Maud, was born on 3rd April 1900. The family was living in Crown Street when the 1901 census was taken and it shows that Samuel was aged twenty-four and a fruiterer/shopkeeper born Combs, with Harriet his wife aged twenty-six born Stowupland and Doris aged one born Stowmarket; also staying with them was Sam's twelve year old cousin, Laura **Baker** of Wetheringsett. Harriet must have been in the last few weeks of her pregnancy when the census was taken (usually late in March) as Vera Irene was born 21st April 1901, but sadly she died aged twenty-two months in 1903. Also born at Crown Street was Ronald Edward Samuel (Ronnie) on 27th May 1902. However, Wilfred Alphous Jack (Jack) was born at 6 Market Place on the 26th June 1908, as was Leslie Arthur James (Les), born 3rd February 1914.

Right from the start Sam concentrated on building up the business, using only high quality, locally grown produce as well as imported seasonal fruits such as oranges, lemons, grapes, bananas etc. Potatoes and other root crop vegetables like carrots, swedes, turnips, parsnips, beetroot, leeks and onions as well as the green vegetables such as cabbage, sprouts, cauliflower, sprouting broccoli and curly kale, made up the main core of the business. It must be emphasised that the availability of these crops was dependent entirely on the seasons, with salad produce, strawberries and other soft fruit available only during the short summer season. Eggs were also sold, these being less plentiful during the winter months when the hens went off lay. English apples were a vital component of everybody's diet and the various types had different maturing and harvesting times, Beauty of Bath being the earliest, followed by Worcester Pearmain, Cox, Russet, James Grieve and Bramley. These all had a variety of tastes, textures and uses ranging from a sweet eating apple to a sharper cooker. Many people will remember wrapping apples individually in paper 'to lay them up' throughout the winter months, thereby ensuring a continuous supply of the versatile fruit for apple turnovers, pies, tarts and crumbles, not forgetting the ever-popular baked apple that would generally accompany most Sunday lunches.

During the 1930's the business also included flowers and bulbs; wreaths, crosses and sprays were made as well. At this time a thriving wholesale trade was built up with

Burrows' shop captured in photographs of the
"Salute the Soldier Week"
Grand Carnival, Saturday June 17th 1944

Les Burrows in the doorway of his shop

Sam **Burrows'** lorries delivering fruit and potatoes to other businesses in the area. Three Dodge lorries were used for this part of the business and these would have to negotiate the narrow Judges Walk (beside the HSBC bank and the bollards in Wilkes Way) to get to the rear of the Market Place buildings where the storage area was located to enable them to load up. Doris, Ronnie, Jack and Leslie were all involved in the business, so when Sam died on 9th July 1941 aged just sixty-four, the business was able to carry on with Harriet overseeing the whole enterprise.

Ronnie and Jack were mainly responsible for the running of the wholesale business whilst Les looked after the shop. This arrangement continued for over ten years until Ronnie and Jack left the business, which meant that the wholesale side ceased in 1953 and Les took over full share of the business. Les had been a paid pupil at the Grammar School and this grounding stood him in good stead for this vocation. Leslie **Burrows** was married at Helmingham on 25th August 1940 to Joan **Weedon**, who had worked at Olivia's hairdressing salon at the Arcade in Ipswich Street. Joan was one of ten children from Helmingham, her father being the estate manager at Helmingham Hall. Les enlisted in the army and was stationed at Newport, Shropshire and that is where on 21st March 1943 they had twin sons, Anthony Rodney (Tony) and Leslie. Les was later stationed at Shrewsbury and was a corporal in charge of a fuel tanker. During this period he would visit his family, who had moved back to Stowmarket, by travelling on a motorbike. Their third child, Roger, was born in Stowmarket in 1951. During this period the family was helped on a full-time basis in the shop by Dennis **Francis**. Dennis also remembers Mrs

Edwards, wife of the landlord of the Greyhound public house next door, serving in the shop. Dennis left the business early in 1961 and his post was filled by Mrs **Ling**, beginning as temporary staff but quickly becoming full-time, which she continued to do until 1980.

Tony remembers that as a twelve year old schoolboy he helped his father on Saturdays, although he always seemed to be given the dirty jobs such as cleaning, washing and trimming the Fen celery; he also helped to wash and cook the beetroot in the built-in copper at the rear of the shop. Tony started working full-time with his father upon leaving school in 1958. He helped with dressing the windows and fixtures as well as laying out the fruit displays. **Burrows'** had the tenders to supply all the Stowmarket school canteens and Stow Lodge Hospital with potatoes and vegetables, the deliveries being made in an Austin estate car and Tony remembers being given a cup of cocoa in the kitchens of each port of call. He also remembers that although they had to rely on some produce coming from Covent Garden, their purchasing policy was to buy in local produce as far as possible. Their strawberries came from **Waspe's** of Boyton Hall, vegetables including cabbages and sprouts from Harold **Marshall's** at Stowupland and lettuces and tomatoes from **Narey's** and the Danecroft Nursery in Finborough Road. In addition to this, Leslie, who by then lived at 21 Wynton Rise, Needham Road, was able to sell eggs from his own chickens, and home-gown beans and cut chrysanthemums in the shop. Opening hours were from 8:30am to 6:00pm but closed on Tuesday afternoons; as all the shop cleaning was done on Sundays, this showed that Les worked a seven-day week and was reluctant to take any holidays. However, Les' interest outside of work was bowls and he was a long-standing member of the Rookery Bowls Club.

As the shop front was open to the street with their wares on full display, Tony remembers that people, especially children, pinching fruit was a continuous problem. Tony's other personal memories include accidentally leaving the handbrake off in one of the lorries parked in Judges Walk. It free-wheeled across the road and hit into **Preston's** wall on the opposite side of Crowe Street. He also remembers dropping a galvanized pail full of eggs, several of which rolled across the floor and down a passageway. In 1968 Tony decided that the family business did not have sufficient turn-over to support two families and left to manage **Peachey's** fruit and vegetable shop in Brook Street, Ipswich. This arrangement lasted for two years when he then changed his career and went into manufacturing where he has stayed for thirty-three years.

Poppy **Stewart** began working at the shop in 1973 and remembers it being a friendly working atmosphere and she has happy memories of the personal service they provided. Poppy served in the shop alongside Les until his retirement aged sixty-nine in 1983, the shop being sold to **Parkyn's Estate Agency**. However, the shop continued as a fruit and vegetable shop for some while, being run by Len **Burton**, who had married Elizabeth **Ames**, daughter of Fred and Sheila **Ames**, who had the Wolsey Road fruit, vegetable and flower business. Poppy worked for a short while at **Ames**' shop in Wolsey Road with Daphne **Ames** (née **Williams**) but when Len leased the shop from **Parkyn's**, Poppy and Daphne moved to help in the Market Place premises on a part-time basis sharing duties with Pam **Cobbold** and Mrs **Ling**.

Les Burrows just prior to his retirement in 1983

This arrangement continued for about six years until the late 1980's when the fruit and vegetable business finally ceased trading from that premises. The shop became **F1 (Return)** computer business for a short while before **Parkyn's Estate Agents** moved their operation from Ipswich Street into the building they had owned for nearly ten years. ❑

Cooper's Coaches

According to an obituary report of 1953 for Joseph William (Joe) **Cooper**, he was accredited as being one of the first public service vehicle operators in the area in 1908, using just one horse and cart, which ferried people from Battisford and Combs to the Thursday market in Stowmarket, including a special service to provide transportation for the Armistice Sunday Parade in the town after the end of the First World War.

Joseph William was born at Battisford in 1872, son of James and Elizabeth (Betsey) **Cooper** (née **Disney**). James died in April 1881 aged forty-five, so in the 1881 census taken later the same month, Betsey was listed as a widow aged forty-five, born at Battisford, with sons James aged eighteen, agricultural labourer, Walter aged fourteen, Henry aged eleven and Joseph aged eight, all scholars. On August 11th 1900, Joseph, aged twenty-five, married Kate Emily Ethel **Thing**, aged twenty-three, daughter of Robert **Thing** (deceased) at **Webb's** School Room, Combs according to the rites of the Congregational Chapel. They first lived in a thatched cottage which served as the Post Office in the parish of Battisford where some of the family were born.

Joseph William (Joe) Cooper

They later moved to Goddard's Farm, a small-holding of forty acres, which although directly opposite their first cottage, was in the parish of Combs. This was where the rest of the children were subsequently born. These were Muriel Ellen (Nellie) born 18th May 1901, Amos Major born 9th March 1903, John Harold born 1st March 1905, Wilfred (Wilf) born 16th June 1908, Frederick William born 2nd February 1911, Elizabeth Miriam May (Betty) born 18th May 1913, Mary Kathleen born 5th March 1915, Edna born 22nd May 1917 and Joan Sylvia born 14th January 1920. However, on each occasion Joseph was listed as a fowl dealer. Joseph's brother, Henry, married Emma **Welham** on the 10th November 1893 at Battisford and had children Archer (Archie) born 31st August

Kate Emily Ethel Cooper (née Thing)

AH 7328, a solid-tyred coach circa 1920

1894, Russell C. born 17th March 1905 and Augustus born 19th April 1914; on each occasion Henry was listed as a carrier.

The early services began in a very basic way according to the memories of Edward John **Waspe**. Quoting from a chapter entitled "Memories of a full and enjoyable life" in the *"Chronicles of Ringshall"* by Maureen **Wills:** "There was one means of transport in those early 1920's, Joe **Cooper's** pig lorry. The first passenger service for the villages of Battisford, Ringshall, Little Finborough and Combs. This same lorry that had transported livestock to market for auction had now been cleaned out of its straw and pig manure, some form of seating had been installed from stools for the passengers. There was still a smell of pigs but what did that matter they were getting a ride into Stow. Also a very bumpy ride over the granite stones and holes. I believe it had solid tyres. For the passengers to board the lorry was nearly as much problem as we had loading the livestock. The half back board had to be let down, and Joe **Cooper** would bring along a pair of steps for the passengers to climb up into the lorry, and a helping hand would given by someone already in". Edward goes on to say that the lorry was almost completely blacked out as there were no windows, so someone would have to give a running commentary by explaining that "We're now going past Combs butchers" or "Now going past the Live and Let Live" and so on."

The Cooper Family
(back row)(l. to r.) Father Joe, Wilf, Betty (looking over Mary's shoulder) and Fred
(front row)(l. to r.) Edna, Mary and Joan

In the Kelly's directories of 1916 and 1922, H. **Cooper** is listed as the carrier to Combs from the Duke's Head in Stowmarket every Thursday. In the 1925 Kelly's it lists Joseph **Cooper** as carrier 'from the Duke's Head Thursdays and Saturdays' and in the Combs section, Joseph is also running a 'service from Combs to Ipswich on Tuesdays'. By 1933, under the heading of carriers from Stowmarket, are listed: To Battisford and Combs on Thursdays, **Cooper** from King's Head. To Combs on Thursdays and Saturdays, Joseph **Cooper**, from Market Place. In the Battisford listing, Joseph is classified as a carrier and as sub-postmaster, a post which he held until 1938. Henry was listed as a smallholder and Mrs Emma **Cooper**, a shopkeeper. Joe's obituary also states that he was for many years a drummer with the Battisford Mission Band and had been associated with local preaching all his working life.

Wilfred (Wilf) Cooper

Joan (left) and Betty Cooper, standing in front of the family's Morris Commercial coach

In 1937 **Cooper's** service covered Battisford, Wattisham, Ringshall, Bricett and Combs from the King's Head, Stowmarket, on Thursdays, Saturdays and Sundays. From April 1st 1937, Wattisham airfield was being constructed in readiness for the developments in Germany which were to lead to the Second World War. Local labour was used to build the site with men coming in from all the surrounding towns and villages. By the time of its completion in May 1939, two squadrons of Blenheim medium range bombers had taken up residence and Wattisham camp's buildings had been occupied by many of the servicemen who had come into the area.

Cooper's Coaches would play an important role in the morale of the men by ferrying them into Stowmarket for their provisions as well as their wider social needs. **Cooper's** never had their

"The Night Hawks"
Fred (left) and Wilf (with cigarette)

Fred (in uniform) and Amos Cooper
outside Stowmarket Railway Station

Ronnie Smith standing by Bedford Duple coach HBJ 750

Wilf Cooper beside LGV 555

own livery, as the buses were usually bought second-hand from other companies and kept what ever colour they were delivered with; many people may remember a bus that was known as the 'Green Pea' because of its pea-green paintwork. Other colours included a slate grey coach with a pink stripe as well as a blue coach with a cream stripe. Fred, Amos and Wilf, sons of Joe, were all drivers for the company, although they also used to work at their parents' farm and drove farm trucks. When Amos married Blanche Annie **Stiff**, daughter of Arthur Turner **Stiff**, on February 12th 1930, he was described as motor bus driver and when Wilf married Kathleen Blanche **Fayers**, daughter of Robert **Fayers**, on 21st June 1940 he was an omnibus driver.

The main core of the daily business consisted of being under contract to East Suffolk County Council to deliver and collect local children to and from their respective schools. Further services included the daily shopping runs leaving at 9:00am to return at 1:00pm and the afternoon run leaving at 2:00pm and returning at 4:00pm. Evening services departed at 6:00pm and 7:00pm and returned at 10:00pm and 11:00pm, giving villagers and servicemen the chance to enjoy the social facilities offered at the Regal and Palladium cinemas and local public houses. The coaches during this period were often standing room only, as the servicemen would fill every available space to attend dances and special functions in the town at venues such as the Constitutional Club in Milton Road and the Corn Exchange in the Market Place.

After the end of the war and into the early 1950's, the availability of excursions became more accessible due to the easing of petrol rationing. Destinations included the seaside resorts of Felixstowe, Clacton-on-Sea, Great Yarmouth and Southend to see the lights. Regular trips were also made to London Kings Cross and Ipswich. Other places further afield gradually became included such as Birmingham and Coventry and also as far as Scotland. Local darts teams were taken to 'away' matches all over the county. This was

Wilf Cooper (left) and Alec Tollhurst, circa 1950

considered to be the peak period for the company and three coaches were in continual use, being Bedford Duples and a Guy. Other drivers who worked for the company were Ronnie **Smith**, who used to live near to Wattisham gate-house, who unfortunately died just before he was due to be married, Arthur **Sparkes**, Mr **Keeble**, Alec **Tollhurst**, Gerry **Bluet** and Tommy **Doe**. The coaches used to have conductors to collect the money, cardboard tickets being issued and this also was kept in the family to some degree as Betty **Buckle**, sister to Amos, Wilf and Fred, was licensed to drive a small bus. She was also a conductress as was Ivy **Cooper**, now **Bailey**, niece to Joseph and daughter of Archer H. **Cooper** (Archie) and Ettie (née **Pearl**). Ivy, who became Wilf's second wife in 1958, was also his second-cousin-once-removed.

Although Mary **Cooper**, daughter of Joseph and Kate, did not work for the company, she enjoyed the benefits of free travel, especially into Stowmarket where she worked. However, she found that she was drawn in to perform extra small duties in order to help out on some occasions. This involved taking a serviceman who had missed the bus, which had left a few minutes early, from Wattisham Guardroom into Stowmarket. Another time one of the coaches ran out of petrol at nearby Barking, necessitating her to ferry a can of petrol in her car to enable the coach to complete its journey. Mary could remember that sometimes in extreme weather conditions the bus could not always get through, although she can never remember there being any accidents. She also commented

COOPER'S COACHES
COMBS

Daily Service: Stowmarket - Wattisham (R.A.F.) via Combs, Battisford and Ringshall

Excursions from Market Place to:—

LONDON (Theatre and Coach Ticket combined)

SUFFOLK SHOW and SUMMER EXCURSIONS

REGULAR EXCURSION to IPSWICH FOOTBALL (Home Matches) Depart Combs Ford Corner (Magpie Inn) one hour before kick-off.

Coaches for private hire all occasions

'Phone Stowmarket 103

Cooper's advertisment on page 18 of the 1955 Edition of 'Newby's Stowmarket Annual Guide & Directory'

on the fact that the buses used by the servicemen were usually 'noisily boisterous' but generally well-behaved.

In 1957, **Cooper's** Coaches was bought by **Mulley's** of Ixworth and was renamed Combs Coaches, so called because of the area it covered and all the coaches were given cream and orange livery. This service continued for several more years and many people will remember the old wooden ticket office on the Duke's Head car-park from where excursions were advertised and advance tickets sold.

Kate, widow of Joseph, died on 3rd November 1970 aged ninety-four, having worked very hard all her life by sewing and making clothes for the children and taking in extra washing. She was sub-postmistress for about thirty years, during which time letters were brought from Stowmarket by a postman on a bicycle. Right up to the end of her life, Kate kept herself busy by knitting and sewing items that were sold at bazaars and coffee mornings in the village.

Wilfred **Cooper** died 6th September 1977 aged sixty-nine whilst taking part in a band concert at Saffron Walden, Essex.

Mary **Cooper** died in 2002 and Edna **Cooper** died in 2003. ❑

14 STOWMARKET ANNUAL, 1959

For all Your Coach Travel

IT'S CHEAPER AND BETTER

by

COMBS COACHES LTD.

STOWMARKET

Over Thirty Coaches and Super 41-seater Tourers

New Excursions for the 1959 Season

Telephone: Pakenham 234 and Stowmarket 560

(above) Combs Coaches advertised in a 1959 street directory and (right) in a 1969/70 edition

Travel in comfort by . . .

Combs Coaches Ltd.

STOWMARKET

Office: REGAL CAR PARK	LUXURY 52 - 45 - 41 - 29 SEATER COACHES FOR HIRE	'Phone: 2865

QUOTATIONS WITHOUT OBLIGATION

ANYWHERE - ANYTIME

Daily Excursions during the summer to:

FELIXSTOWE CLACTON
YARMOUTH, Etc.

Also long day tours to:

LONDON AIRPORT & WINDSOR, NORTH WALES, LONDON and WHIPSNADE ZOOS, STATELY HOMES.

These are only a few !

See our Advertisments in Stowmarket Chronicle for full list

TRY OUR POPULAR SUNDAY EVENING MYSTERY TOURS - ONLY 3/9

A painting by Essex artist Malcolm Root showing a Leyland PSI coach turning onto the Duke's Head car park reminding us of a scene which would have been common circa 1960. The coach was brought from St Albans by Joseph Cooper and originally had a grey and red livery before changing to the cream and orange colours of Combs Coaches. *(By kind permission of the artist)*

HAIRDRESSERS

Day's

The building currently occupied by the Estate Agents, **Hamilton Smith** Stowmarket Ltd., trading as Stowmarket Mortgage Centre, is a 16th century timber-framed building that may have been the original Queen's Head Inn as found in an old advertisement in the 'Bury and Norwich Post' dated 1793, housed at the Ipswich Record Office. This states that the Queen's Head was situated "on the junction of Ipswich, Bury and Stowupland Streets (now Station Road) and opposite Finborough Road". Capone's (ex-Queen's Head) is now further back from the junction and is a much later building (early Victorian). However, the old building 2-4 Bury Street seems to have been used as a barbers throughout most of the nineteenth and twentieth centuries, as can be followed through old directories. It may go back as far as 1823 when Charles **Langham** had a hairdressing salon in Bury Street, but the first positively known placement was in the 1870's when **Druce's** occupied the site and it appears on some early photographs.

Druce's were there until 1900 and continued to own the premises when, in a 1912 Kelly's directory, Mr Horace **Huckleby** ran the business. In 1916 he was followed by Mr Thomas E. **Kerridge** and in the 1925 Kelly's directory it belonged to George **Smith**, all of these appearing as hairdressers. In the early 1930's Robert Edgar (Eddie) **Day** bought the business from Mr **Smith** whilst continuing to rent the premises from Mrs Harriet **Druce**, until 1940 when the **Day** family eventually bought the property, which also included the next-door premises at number six. This was Mr J. W. **Tippler's** umbrella repair shop and book and bible shop and he became a tenant of Eddie **Day** until he eventually moved his business further up the road to 24 Bury Street to take over Mrs Alice **Purkis'** wool and fancy goods shop, becoming known as the Bible Shop (currently Stowmarket Bookshop). The flat above Mr **Tippler's** was at that time rented by Miss **Hunnibell**, but after she died the flat was used as live-in accommodation by the manageress of the ladies' hairdressing salon. Numbers 2, 4, and 6 became R. E. **Day's** Gents and Ladies Hairdresser, tobacconist and boutique for over thirty years.

Robert Edgar (Eddy) Day & Mabel (née Farrow) circa 1950

It is recorded in the family that both of Robert's parents had worked for the **Duke of Grafton** on the Euston estate, with John, who had a deep love of horses, working, probably as a farrier and Ellen as a lady's maid, which would explain how they met. After they were married they lived for a while in the Euston Lodge Cottage. However, as soon as she became pregnant, she would have had to leave the household, as was the custom in those days. Robert Edgar (Eddie) **Day** was born in Bridge Street, Stowmarket on the 13th April 1880, son of John Edgar **Day** and Ellen (née **Hayes**). On the 1881 census he appears at Lime Tree Place/Bridge Street as an eleven month old baby. Father, John, is listed as a thirty-five year old blacksmith, born Stowmarket, Ellen was twenty-two, born Euston (near Thetford) and they had two boarders, John **Bridgeman** aged thirty-five and his six year old son George (who were employed by the **Day** family). By the 1891 census John and Ellen were ten years older and John was listed as a dairyman (John later sold the dairy to **Thurlow and Sons** dairy business), Robert was a ten year old scholar and the family also consisted of George born 1883, Violet born 1884, John R. (it has been a family tradition to have the name John in every generation) born 1888, William born 1891 and Frederick born 1893 (and it is Frederick's son John, born in Vancouver, Canada, who continues that tradition).

When he married on the 27th December 1909, Robert Edgar **Day** was aged twenty nine and gave his occupation as a dairyman, working for his father. His bride was twenty-one year old Mabel **Farrow** (Robert's brother George married Mabel's sister May, daughters of Joseph **Farrow**, who ran a market-garden business from land that later became allotments in Takers Lane) of Mabel Cottage, 1 Takers Lane. George and Frederick later emigrated to Canada.

Robert and Mabel's first child, Dorothy Olive was born 15th November 1910, John Ronald was born 3rd January 1912, Nellie Kathleen (Kathleen) was born 3rd October 1913, Margaret Joan (Peggy) was born 20th February 1915. They were all born at 99/101 Lime Tree Place, which was also the Post-Office and general store. By the time that Raymond was born at Mabel Cottage, Takers Lane on 14th June 1919, the Post Office, stores and property had passed to Thomas J. **Waspe**. John Edgar **Day**, Robert's father, died at 84 Bridge Street and was buried on 17th December 1929 aged eighty-three.

Edgar Day's Post Office and shop in Lime Tree Place circa 1915

When Robert was aged fifty-four in 1934, R. E. **Day's** hairdressing shop first appears in one of the town's business directories, with the gentlemen's department being situated on the ground floor of 2, Bury Street. Robert, who combined managing the business with his love of being a lay-preacher, hired skilled hairdressers and was able to provide training for his son, Raymond, in the hairdressing trade. Daughter Kathleen learnt her skills in London and at the age of twenty-one was able to set up her ladies' salon upstairs above the gents' salon with its entry from 4, Bury Street. Also during this period their brother, John, began to receive local acclaim for his dance band known as 'Jack **Day's** Dance Band' (see photograph page 24). The gents hairdressing staff started at 8:30am (finishing at 5:30 pm) which was before most of the other businesses that started their day at 9:00 am. Many of the businessmen used to go to the hairdresser's for their morning shave, so it would not be hard to imagine many business deals and gossip being exchanged whilst being lathered up awaiting the first pass of the cut-throat razor.

Robert (Eddie) and Mabel Day's children taken at Robinson's Studio in Ipswich Street (l. to r.) Dorothy, John, Kathleen and Peggy

Robert continued managing the business with Kathleen, throughout the war years, as both Raymond and John were called up to serve in the Forces. At the end of the war, when Robert retired, Raymond again came back to his position in the family business. On the day in 1941 when the bomb fell on the Congregational Church in Ipswich Street, its minister, the Reverend **Weir**, was in the shop chatting to Robert over a cup of tea. As the sirens sounded and they heard the plane approaching, they managed to pull some people off the street and get them down into the cellar under the shop. Kathleen was upstairs with other members of staff rushing around and switching off electrical equipment etc. and had no time to join the others in the cellar. During this period the

A Day's advertisement from the 1930's

Hello Everybody!

R. E. DAY

Hairdresser and Tobacconist :

2 & 4 BURY STREET,
Opposite Automatic Signals.

STOP	All kinds of Tobacco and Cigarettes.
WALK IN	Brilliantines a Speciality.
GO OUT PLEASE	Blades of all good Brands in Stock From 1d. each.

Our Crops are looking s-well

Day's advertisement in a 1931 'Shopping Week' pamphlet making reference to the new traffic light system at the Bury Street/Market Place/Tavern Street/ Station Road crossroads

gents' department had six seats and the day to day running of the salon was by Messrs **Hayward** and **Wheaton**.

Robert, who was a lay-preacher at the Congregational Church, also gave services in the surrounding villages chapels, such as Battisford, Buxhall, Finborough, Haughley and Elmswell. He was also a Boys' Brigade Officer as well as being a well-respected Superintendent of the two Sunday Schools and was naturally very upset at the loss of such a fine building, especially the ceiling of the upper school which was covered in hand-painted texts. Mabel, too, played her part in church life by running the Bible Class and supervising the flower arranging for all services and special festivals. Kathleen recalls that there were two big events at the church that her father would always be very involved with and remembered for: the first was the Anniversary Sunday when the church was filled with parents and children who had practised for weeks singing special hymns and the other was the Sunday School outing to Felixstowe by train.

During the war period Robert, who was also much involved with the Y.M.C.A. in the town, would invite personnel from the Berkshire Regiment and later the American servicemen who were stationed in the town, back to his home for meals and Kathleen remembers that their house was always full at Christmas time. It was during this period that Kathleen taught hairdressing to City and Guilds standards to students at Ipswich Civic College in its early years. In 1947, Kathleen married Captain Jerry **Reid** at the Savoy Hotel in London and moved to Ipswich to live, as her husband, a stock-broker, commuted to the London Stock Exchange each day. Kathleen continued to run the Stowmarket business

A 1950's photograph of 2, 4 & 6 Bury Street when it was Day's hairdressing establishment with the ladies' department upstairs

Jerry and Kathleen (Kay) Reid

and later also opened up a second salon in Lavenham, which is now owned by one of her former apprentices.

When Robert died at Takers Lane on 15th October 1957 aged seventy-seven, Raymond

A close-up of the ornate glass door panel which led to the ladies hairdressing department and boutique

decided that he did not want to carry on in that trade and so moved, with his mother, to Thorndon and took over the local Post Office and village store. Later on, as his mother's health deteriorated, Raymond and Mabel moved to St Osyth in Essex and Raymond established his own hairdressing business nearby in Little Clacton, until his retirement. Kathleen took over full running of both aspects of the Stowmarket business and traded as Kathleen **Day** Limited. During the 1950's Kathleen had up to four professional hairdressers plus two or three apprentices, one receptionist and herself upstairs in the ladies' department. After Mr **Tippler** had moved his business, that part of the premises became a reception office and a cosmetic boutique which sold jewellery and handbags as well as make-up and stockings. (During the war the scarceness of these items caused long queues to form in Bury Street when word got round that **Day's** had things like 'lipstick or stockings' in stock.) There was also a chiropody department and a staff kitchen. In 1946 Kathleen and her staff won a silver cup for 'Hairstylist of the Year' covering the counties of Norfolk, Suffolk and Cambridgeshire. In 1950, Kathleen obtained in London a Trichology Diploma which greatly enhanced the services offered to the clients. During the 1950's, the gents' business was completely modernised and

Phone : Stowmarket 224

KATHLEEN DAY LTD.

LADIES' & GENT'S HAIR STYLISTS

2, 4 & 6 BURY STREET

STOWMARKET

Managing Director : **K. REID**

An appointment card from the 1950's

Raymond Day

managed by Mr **Cresswell**; Kathleen also recalls that the gents' department had a lady hairdresser by the name of 'Happy' **Chapman**, who proved to be very good for business during her stay with them.

Kathleen states that during the war and for some time afterwards, the business had the contract to cut the hair of the airmen in the Officers' Mess at RAF Wattisham and remembers that on several occasions when an alert was sounded, the men would have to rush out and man their planes with only a half a haircut. She added that this was always rectified as soon as possible at a later date. **Day's** sometimes had occasion to produce wigs for some servicemen at the RAF camp who had suffered hair loss as a result of accidents or burns etc. Throughout most of its history, the gents' business had just been a 'sit and wait your turn' barber's shop but Kathleen introduced an appointment system and upgraded the service to include cutting, shampooing and blow-drying etc. At this time there were three professional hairdressers each with an apprentice.

Sadly, Kathleen's husband, Jerry, died in 1961 aged only forty-seven, but she carried on running her business for a few more years before selling the business and the properties to Mr **Berriman** in 1968 and moving to Lilliput, overlooking Poole harbour in Dorset. Mr **Berriman** incorporated the hairdressing business with the **Wilden's** newsagency and tobacconists next door at 8 Bury Street so that for several years numbers 2 - 8 all carried the **Wilden's** name. ❑

Jack Day's Dance Band

Durrant's

NEWSAGENT & STATIONER

Roughly where the entrance to QD Stores is now situated, used to be the site of **Durrant's** newsagent and tobacconist shop. The premises, which became 9 Ipswich Street after properties were required to be identified by numbering in circa 1908, had previously been owned by the **Woolby** family, dating back to a reference in an 1844 Whites directory which has the entry under Booksellers '**Woolby** Thos (printer, newsagent, stamp vendor, etc) Ipswich Street. The listing as stamp vendor is interesting as stamps had first been issued for payment for mail only two years earlier, so the shop would have been one of the first in the area to deal with the early 'Penny Blacks'. Thomas Bracket **Woolby**, postmaster, died January 3rd 1862 aged eighty-three; his son Arthur then took over the running of the business. Arthur then suffered the loss of his wife Elizabeth Mary on June 20th 1868 aged only thirty-three. The 1881 census shows the **Woolby** family consisting of Arthur B a widow aged fifty-two, printer, bookseller etc. with children: Ellen E, governess aged twenty-two, William A, printer aged twenty-one, Annie M shop assistant (bookseller) aged sixteen, Emily C aged fourteen and Edith J aged thirteen, both scholars, plus Eliza, postmistress aged fifty-three and Jane housekeeper aged fifty-one, both sisters to Arthur, all born in Stowmarket. Also Martha aged sixty-seven, a cousin visiting from Ipswich, as well as Alice **Ruddock**, an eighteen year old domestic servant. Arthur Bracket **Woolby** appears in many of the various directories to 1885 as printer, stationer, bookseller and stamp distributor alongside his sister Miss Eliza **Woolby** as postmistress. By 1900 the business was being run by two of Arthur's daughters, Annie and Emily, who continued up until 1916, as can be found in the Kelly's directory of the time, along with the entry for Henry **Durrant** at number 12 Ipswich Street (now the British Heart Foundation charity shop, formerly 'Poundsaver', 'Breakers' and Meesons), which prior to that date had been owned by Walter **Beckwith**. Walter and Emma **Beckwith** appear on the 1881 census in Ipswich Street. Walter is listed as being a stationer aged thirty-eight from

ARTHUR B. WOOLBY,

BOOKSELLER, PRINTER, AND STATIONER,

STOWMARKET,

In presenting thanks to his Friends and the Public for their favours, assures them it is a great pleasure to find their kind wishes expressed on his taking the business, and seconded in so substantial a manner, are proved to be still felt, by an *increased* patronage during the past year, and will endeavour to show his appreciation of the same, by supplying them with every article in the Trade of the best quality on the most reasonable Terms.

Having made considerable additions to his stock of Printing Materials, he is enabled to execute Printing of every description in an improved style.

Each Books, Ledgers, & other Account Books.

PENS, INKS, &c. &c.

CREAM LAID NOTE, 5 Quires $7\frac{1}{2}$d. to 3s.

ENVELOPES 6d, and 1s. per 100.

COPY BOOKS NOT SURPASSED AT THE PRICES.

Bibles, Prayer Books, and Church Services.

London and Country Newspapers supplied.

Books and Periodicals regularly procured from London Twice a Week.

An advertisement from 1856

Henry Durrant (left) with Alfred Cole

This caricature of Henry Durrant by 'Matt' appeared along with other 'Stowmarket Celebrities' in the Sunday Graphic & Sunday News on 9th December 1934

Maldon in Essex and his wife aged forty from Colchester, Essex. By 1922 Henry, who had previously worked at the **W. H. Smith** and Son newspaper kiosk on Stowmarket Station, had also bought 9 Ipswich Street from the **Woolby** sisters. Henry ran both 9 and 12 Ipswich Street for several years.

Henry **Durrant** had been born on the 14th January 1875 at Southrepps in Norfolk and he appears aged six on the 1881 census living in Church Street, Southrepps with his grandparents James **Durrant**, aged forty-two, farm labourer born Hanworth, Norfolk and Priscilla, aged forty-nine, wife, born Aylsham, Norfolk. By 1901 Henry had already arrived in Stowmarket where he is listed as a twenty-six

Henry Durrant at the wheel of his car in circa 1940. In the passenger seat is Mrs Chambers. Barbara Grey is standing beside Henry with William Grey opposite

In the rear garden of 'Kettelea' 7 Finborough Road, the house Henry had built in the 1930's. Henry Durrant is seated at the table with Mrs Chambers on the right of the picture.

year old Book-Stall Clerk lodging in Unity Road with Ernest **Chambers,** a thirty-two year old Railway Clerk, and **Esther** his wife of the same age. At the outbreak of the First World War, Henry was forty-two and along with many others enlisted in the army and saw service abroad. During his absence his shop and business was managed by Mr and Mrs **Chambers**; Mrs **Chambers** also carried on as his housekeeper after he moved to live over his shop. Henry's niece, Mrs Barbara Joan **Denny** (née **Gray**), remembers visiting him at his home above the shop at 9 Ipswich Street in the 1930's and how she used to get the remnants of wedding receptions from Mayhew's the bakery next door, brought round by Doris **Mayhew**. Barbara also remembers her uncle being a "lovely and jovial man with a great circle of friends"; he also enjoyed many sports including cricket, fishing and shooting and was a founder member of the Rookery Bowls Club. In the late 1930's, in preparation for his retirement, Henry bought a piece of land in Finborough

From a 1930 Stowmarket Guide Book

Road where he built his house. He sold the plots either side of his house 'so he could choose his neighbours' and two more houses were subsequently built by Messrs **Cole** and **Hart**.

In a Stowmarket Shopping Week, Official Programme dated Thursday 11th to Saturday 20th June 1931, the entry for H **Durrant** reads: "9 and 12 Ipswich Street, the Fountain Pen Hospital, for Leather and Fancy Goods, Stationery. Newspapers and Magazines delivered in the town and surroundings". The same pamphlet also invited the public to guess the number of articles displayed in the window of number 12 Ipswich Street shop, the best three guesses would be awarded prizes of goods valued at five shillings 5/- (25p), three shillings 3/- (15p) and two shillings 2/- (10p). The 12 Ipswich Street building dealt purely with the newsagency business and was shared with a sweetshop managed by Mrs Ida **Cole**, **Durrant's** occupying the corner position with a window in **Marriott's** Walk. Mrs Beryl **Norman** (née **Pettit**), who worked there for about eighteen months from 1938, remembers earning five shillings per week (5/-) (25p) which included working from 8:00am to 8:00pm on Saturdays to cope with the sales of the 'Green-Un' and 'Pink-Un' sports results papers. Beryl says that she was just one of two women working in the shop, the other being Mrs Joyce **Anderson** (née **Brame**). They had to negotiate very "narrow rickety old stairs" to get to the upstairs room where the cigarettes were stored. There also used to be a booking office for seats at the Regal Cinema and Beryl says that they had to be careful not to over-book any particular day's performance during what was a very popular period for films. About fifty to

The Ipswich Street Store (with car outside) in the 1950's

sixty newspapers were posted to outlying customers in the surrounding villages and farms; this involved rolling them in papers to be got ready for posting and covering an area reaching almost to Bury St Edmunds. There were about five or six paperboys who also did morning local deliveries and about the same number that did the 'Evening Star' rounds.

In 1938 Henry **Durrant** retired; he lived at 7 Finborough Road until his death in June the following year aged sixty-four. The business had been purchased from Henry by Mr Arthur **Moore**, born 10th June 1894, son of William Vincent **Moore** and his wife Agnes (née **Carse)** from Wilton near Salisbury, Wiltshire. Arthur's grandfather, father and brother had all been Mayor of Wilton, a post later held by his niece. Arthur **Moore** was an imaginative, entrepreneurial type who raised his initial capital to enter the news trade by winning a substantial amount of money from newspaper prize crossword competitions, which were a regular feature of the 1930's press. He even wrote a book

Margery and Arthur Moore January 1954 at their daughter Pamela's wedding to John Rolfe, with Sheila in the background as bridesmaid

Margery and Arthur Moore with their daughters Sheila Valente (née Moore) (l.) and Pamela Dent (late Rolfe née Moore) (r)

June 1957 at Sutton on Sea, Lincs. (l. to r.) Sheila, Arthur holding Pamela's baby daughter Penelope, Pamela and Margery

Durrant's shop at No 9 Ipswich Street circa 1969-70, which was situated in between No 5 Boots the Chemists (original position)(l) and No 11 Mayhew's confectioners (r)

entitled 'How I win at Crosswords' which was very popular at the time. His move to Suffolk was influenced by the fact that Stowmarket was on the main railway line from London to Norwich, which would later facilitate a direct supply of news publications from London publishers. From 1938 to 1940, Arthur **Moore**, his wife Margery (née **Shepherd**) and two daughters, Sheila and Pamela, lived over the shop until he purchased 23 Temple Road.

The business retained the name **Durrant's** and continued to operate from the Ipswich Street premises, where display stands with a large range of newspaper, magazine and periodical titles appeared at No.9 for the first time. Arthur **Moore** was a pioneer of the concept of self-service in the 1940's at a time when this was uncommon and had a notice which read, "Please walk round, we shall never ask you to buy". With the purchase of the Combs Ford Newsagency the business expanded as the number of patrons and newsrounds increased. Over the years, innumerable news delivery boys and girls were an integral part of the everyday running of the business. In the 1960's some of them participated in the Stowmarket carnival, walking with their news bags (large sturdy cloth satchels), each displaying a huge letter in sequence spelling out the word **Durrant's**. For as long as the company traded, the 'East Anglian Daily Times' was the most popular newspaper in Suffolk, with the 'Daily Express' and 'Daily Mirror' vying for second place from the 1940's to the 1960's and 'The Sun' from the 1970's.

Arthur bought a number of other newsagents' shops, allowing them to trade under their old names; these included **Gould's** of Swaffham and Bildeston News. He also introduced news into Elton House, Needham Market. By providing these outlets with newspapers and other publications **Durrant's** the news wholesaler was born. The wholesale business expanded from the 1940's and by the mid 1960's supplied fourteen retail outlets in Stowmarket, Haughley, Old Newton, Combs village, Finborough, Rattlesden, Needham Market and Stowupland etc. During the Second World War, it also supplied all the local aerodromes. Henry **Durrant's** large barrow for collecting newspaper bundles from the station had soon become obsolete and was replaced by vans for station collection and delivery to agents. All the business was on a strictly six day week basis, as Sunday news wholesaling was then nationally a totally separate trade.

In his early days in Stowmarket, Arthur was active in the town as Chairman of Stowmarket Football Club, a leading member of the Rookery Bowls Club and he was also one of the first volunteers in the Local Defence Volunteers (LDV) and Home Guard. On VE Day in 1945 he donated all the fireworks and arranged the display on the Duke's Head car park. In 1955 Arthur moved to 27 Temple Road, the former home of Mr Walter J. **Smith**, a miller and merchant, who had traded at the mill in Crown Street, which has recently been converted into flats. In the later years when his health prevented him from spending so much time in the business, which by then had become a limited company, more and more of the decisions rested on the shoulders of his younger daughter, Pamela, with the day-to-day organisation being carried out by the very able Mr Lionel **Kent**, who was by then a director of the company.

Sheila initially worked at the I C I Paints Division as secretary to Harvey **Ormes**, the Assistant Works Manager, but in 1956 she moved to Geneva as secretary to the Deputy Secretary General of the United Nations Organisation. In 1961, following promotion, she moved to New York for the United Nations. In 1965 she married her Brazilian husband, Carlos **Valente**, who was a U.S.A. Regional Representative at the Rotary International World Headquarters, where he worked for twenty-nine years before retiring in 1997. They now live on the outskirts of Chicago and have two sons, the elder, Oliver, being Chief Technology Officer of Sprint Incorporated at their headquarters in Overland Park, Kansas and the younger, Rudolfo, an orthodontist in Chicago. Sheila has four grandchildren at present.

Pamela worked with her father after leaving school. Her first husband, John **Rolfe**, was killed in 1958 in Singapore, as pilot of a Canberra bomber, leaving her with a two year old daughter and another on the way. In 1961 she married John **Dent** a chartered civil engineer by whom she had a third daughter. Whilst staying with his own profession, John

60 THE STOWMARKET ANNUAL, 1939.

H. DURRANT,
(A. MOORE.)
9 & 12 IPSWICH STREET,
STOWMARKET

STATIONER - NEWSAGENT
Wholesale & Retail TOBACCONIST

OFFICES supplied at lowest possible rates

The House for
STATIONERY - - LEATHER
FANCY GOODS AND GIFTS

Newspapers and Magazines delivered in the Town and Neighbourhood prompt and regular

The Hospital for
All Makes of FOUNTAIN PENS
Telephone 122.

gradually became more involved in the news business from the late 1960's, particularly after Pamela had purchased the Stowupland newsagency from Mr Leonard **Seaman**. At this time John, Pamela and family moved into 27 Temple Road and later, upon Mr **Kent's** retirement, John became a director of **Durrant's** (Stowmarket) Ltd.

Following the death of Arthur **Moore** in 1968, Pamela **Dent** became Chairman and Managing Director of the company and in doing so became one of only two women in the country running a wholesale weekday newspaper distribution organisation. She sold the retail business at Combs Ford and concentrated on the company business at Ipswich Street. The premises had by then become inadequate with deliveries especially difficult, when it must be remembered that Ipswich Street was then part of the A45 trunk road, the only route from the Midlands to the continent via Felixstowe. It was therefore decided to split the business moving the wholesale part into temporary premises in Bond Street whilst leaving the retail shop at 9 Ipswich Street, until the redevelopment of the east side of the street in 1971, when the goodwill was sold to a new owner opposite in new premises at 10 Ipswich Street. The wholesale business was then expanded and moved to the former Stowmarket Co-operative Society grocery warehouse in Station Road, where there was adequate space for sorting, storing, vehicle garaging and deliveries by large articulated lorries. This building, now known as 'Navigation Wharf', has changed its appearance and usage during its long life. Originally only the ground floor was brick built, the rest of the building being weather boarded with a high pitched roof. It appears in an etching of the river Gipping by H. **Davy** dating from 1838 with a small caption below it describing it as 'Mr **Cowell's** warehouse'. When the upper storey was replaced by factory bricks topped with a lower pitched roof is uncertain, but it was

Tel. Stowmarket 613122 (STD 0449)

OUR REF.

DURRANTS (STOWMARKET) LTD.
Established over 135 years

YOUR REF.

WHOLESALE NEWSPAPER DISTRIBUTORS
Members P.W.N.D.A.

Registered Office : STATION ROAD, STOWMARKET, SUFFOLK. IP14 1AJ

Directors: Mrs. P. M. Dent (Managing) L. W. Kent — Registered No.583188 England

Two views of Pam Dent's Stowupland shop

probably undertaken by the 'Co-op' in the earlier part of the twentieth century. It was further transformed into small business units in the 1990's. By 1985 Pamela had increased the wholesale distribution to twenty-eight retail outlets covering central Suffolk from Wyverstone in the north to Hadleigh in the south and from the A140 in the east to Rattlesden in the west. This involved the business being open seventeen hours a day for six days a week and employing a full and part-time staff of eighteen.

In April 1987 the business was sold to **W. H. Smith** & Son Ltd., the national news wholesalers. John retired in 1991 and by 1992, with the disposal of their Stowupland shop, all business interests had finished and Pamela and John were fully retired and were able to see much more of their three daughters: Penelope, Jane and Julia. Penelope (née **Rolfe**) was formerly a nursing sister at Addenbrookes Hospital, now working for BUPA and is married to David **Salmon**, a chartered civil engineer and chartered loss adjuster. Jane (née **Rolfe**) formerly worked for the probation service but now runs her own internet dating agency business 'nomorefrogs.co.uk' and is married to Michael **Spencer**, production editor at Professional Engineering Publishing (publishers to the Institute of Mechanical Engineers). Julia **Dent** is a professional librarian and keen musician, who holds a Masters degree. They were also able to spend more time with their grand-daughters Rebecca and Vanessa **Salmon** and grandsons Max and Laurence **Spencer**.

Pamela and John **Dent** continued to live at 27 Temple Road until 2001 when sadly John, who despite ill-health, supplied much of this text, died in June aged seventy. In November of that year Pamela moved from Temple Road to a new home in Needham Market. ❑

MEN'S & BOYS'OUTFITTER

Gordon L Ince

Born 14th March 1916 at his parents' General Store in 'The Row' at Hartest near Bury St. Edmund's, Gordon Leslie **Ince** was brought up in an atmosphere where he was quickly able to learn his skills as a shopkeeper and salesman in the grocery and drapery trade. His father, Oscar Harry **Ince**, had served a year of his apprenticeship as an improver at **Turner & Co.** in the Market Place in Stowmarket before marrying Hannah Mary **Theobold** at Methwold, Norfolk. Hannah was from a farming family based at Ten Mile Bank in the Fens; both Hannah, born 1882, and Oscar, born 1877, were from large families. The 1881 census shows the Ince family originated from Shimpling naming John C. **Ince** aged forty-five, born Hartest, carpenter and farmer of forty-nine acres employing four men and one boy, his wife Jane aged forty, born Shimpling and children John W. aged 18, carpenter, George D. aged sixteen, farmer's son and Jane E. aged twelve, scholar, all born in Hartest. Kate S. aged eleven, Ellen M. aged ten, William A. aged seven, Herbert A. aged five, Oscar H. aged three and Bertha L. aged one were all born in Shimpling. Another son, Walter, aged fourteen, born Hartest, was living with his aunt and uncle, Daniel and Sarah **Cooper**, at their farm in Brockley.

Gordon was one of twin boys but unfortunately his brother, Hessle, died soon after being born. His elder brothers, Morley and Kenneth, went to Earls Colne Grammar School in Essex, but Gordon was educated, first at the village school in Hartest and then at Glemsford until he was sixteen. Part of the normal family routine on Sundays was to travel by pony and trap to Glemsford to attend the Ebenezer Baptist Chapel. A large baker's basket would be filled with food items for the whole family's lunch, a private room having been hired at the local public house; this arrangement then allowed them to attend the afternoon service before returning home.

Before leaving school, Gordon's ambition was to become a cabinetmaker, but due to his father's brother Walter's untimely death, it was decided that he should help his Aunt Rosie in their village shop and Post Office at Felsham. During his two-year apprenticeship there he was paid 2/6d (12½p) per week; he 'lived in' with his aunt during the week and would cycle the thirteen miles back to Hartest at weekends. It was a fairly harsh regime and even if he was just one farthing out when balancing up at the end of the day, it was made clear that it would be deducted from his half-crown. Some of his duties included delivering groceries and drapery items around the village on his trade bike, as well as helping in the shop. In 1934 he went to work for **Mason's** General Grocery Store at Woolpit, a position he held until the outbreak of war.

Gordon joined the Royal Air Force in October 1939 and trained at Holton. He served in the British Expeditionary Force (B.E.F) in France and returned home to England on one of the last boats to leave on the day before the Dunkirk Evacuation (May/June 1940). On 21st September that same year he married Muriel Jean **Steward** (known as Jean), daughter of Gordon and Edith **Steward** (née **Waspe**), at Bradfield Combust Methodist

Chapel. Jean, who was born 29th September 1920, did secretarial training in the office of **W. Plumpton** and Son, a draper's shop in Bury St. Edmunds, under the managerial eye of Mr George **Pemberton**.

Gordon Ince's shop in Church Street Eye was situated in the building on the right-hand side of this photograph, which was taken when it was still 'The Eight Bells' Public House. Beside the church was the Guildhall, used by the head-masters of the adjoining Grammar school which dates back to circa 1495 and closed in 1965

Three months after their marriage, Jean and Gordon moved briefly to Chester where he was stationed on an airbase at Harwarden. Gordon was then posted to Valley in Anglesey where he was in charge of the Ground to Air Firing Range at Carmel Head and Jean ran an aircraft factory's canteen in Chester. After a three year stay in Anglesey, Gordon was posted in February 1945 to Sorrento in Italy, from where he was demobilized in the November of the same year. By this time Jean had moved back to her original family home at Bradfield Combust. After leaving the services, Gordon became a commercial traveller covering eight counties, including as far as Birmingham, selling men's clothing, accessories and swimwear. He travelled for ten months and then felt ready to start his own business. Their daughter, Rosemary, was born in September 1946, just prior to their taking over a small grocery, provisions and drapery shop in Church Street, Eye, Suffolk which was used as the tuck shop for Eye Grammar School. He became a borough councillor in 1948 and in 1949, aged just thirty-three, became the youngest Mayor in England when he took the chain of office for the Borough of Eye, a post he held for two years. He was also on the committee that instigated the first of the successful Eye shows. Also in 1949 they bought the old established business of **G. B. Bishop** and Son in the Market Square, which had been there since 1749. Jean ran the smaller shop for less than a year before selling the business and the property. During this period they looked for a larger business and

Gordon Ince in his robes of office leaving Eye Church probably after a mayoral service circa 1950 being congratulated by Canon Donald Rea MBE, vicar of Eye (1934-1966)

(above) Preston Brothers 27 Ipswich Street shop which was bought by Gordon Ince and (below) Preston Bros. letterhead, after the business had been acquired by Gordon Ince in 1953. Note the change in the street numbering from 27 to 25.

Proprietor :
GORDON L. INCE

Preston Bros

Complete
Men's & Boys' Outfitters

Suits to Measure
a Speciality
★
Boots and Shoes

Telephone No. 2087

Only Address :
25 IPSWICH STREET, STOWMARKET

"All goods shown in these windows are available at Gordon L Ince opposite" - the notice displayed on the premises rented by Gordon Ince in Ipswich Street prior to its demolition in the early 1960's

in 1952 they found a suitable grocery shop at Walton near Felixstowe. Their stay there was short but memorable, as they witnessed the great East Coast Floods of January 1953 and Gordon helped by rescuing local people from the roofs of their caravans and prefabs.

In April 1953, Gordon and Jean moved with Rosemary to Stowmarket, buying the **Preston's** menswear premises and business at 25, Ipswich Street from Mr Robert **Preston**. **Preston's** also had another outlet in the town: this was situated on the corner of the Market Place with Crowe Street, currently **Dewhurst** butchers. This part of the business was concerned with drapery, ladies' and children's wear and was run by Robert's brother, Charles.

Gordon, Jean and Rosemary lived above the shop and quickly decided to develop the shop further, enlarging the floor area of the shop by extending the building back to the Church Lane boundary.

Gordon (extreme left) along with other members of Stowmarket Urban District Council assembled in the Market Place in September 1958 for a Sunday 'Battle of Britain' salute

This included purchasing the stables from the Fox Hotel for £100, which enabled them to build up a larger stock and wider range of goods. Mr Stanley **Stannard**, son of the horseman for the **Edwards** family at Rookery Farm, Gipping, had joined **Preston's** at the age of fifteen and was invited to continue his position there under the new ownership. Stanley was able to do this until his retirement at the age of sixty-five, thereby completing fifty years' service. Their stock consisted solely of menswear, ranging from socks to overcoats, suits, casualwear and work clothes, hats, caps, shirts, braces and accessories. Men's and boys' shoes were sold, Dunlop slippers and Wellington boots were also available, the latter being displayed hanging by string on nails at the back of the shop. Hard wearing and industrial strength clothing was also a main concern of the business and Gordon would travel around to various warehouses in Manchester, London, Norwich and Ipswich buying up ex-government service stock for the local farm and foundry workers. Providing a complete range of school uniforms was also another important part of the business that had been founded in their early days. Prices were aimed to suit the working man and country people. Suits costing 49s/11d (£2:50p) were sold, deliberately undercutting Burton's who were known as the 'Fifty-Shilling' tailors. By 1954, a two-chair gents' hairdressing salon was also set up at the rear of the shop with Mr **Perry** the barber, the ploy being that as the men walked through the shop passing the stock displayed, they might be tempted to buy something on their way out. However, provision was also made for workmen in overalls etc. so that they could enter from the Church Lane entrance, thereby not needing to traipse through the shop in their grubby clothes. The shop and especially the salon were rigorously scrubbed and cleaned every three months by a Mrs **Bridgeman** to

PRICE LIST

HAIRCUTTING 2/6

OLD AGE PENSIONERS HALF-PRICE
MONDAY, TUESDAY, WEDNESDAY

BOYS 2/-

HAIRCUT, SHAMPOO & BLOW WAVE 5/6

BLOW WAVE ONLY 1/6

SHAMPOOING

DRY 2/- WET 2/- OIL 2/6

Your custom is appreciated.

If you are satisfied please tell others . .
. . if not please tell us.

The cost of a haircut at Ince's in the 1950's.

help to freshen the place from the effects of the smell of pipes and cigarettes of which many of the clientele partook. By around 1960 a man's haircut would cost one shilling and ninepence (1s/9d) (7p) and a boy's would be sixpence (6d) (2½p). Underwear was wrapped and stored in plain brown paper and Mrs **Ince** remembers the discussions between Gordon and Mr **Stannard** relating to the right and wrong way of re-wrapping these goods: Gordon preferred the grocery trade method which differed from Stanley's clothing and drapery trade method by the way the slip knot was tied. Alterations would be carried out if needed, the items of clothing would be taken by a 'Saturday boy' round to Mr **Whynes** in Milton Road who charged half-a-crown (2s/6d) (12½p) to shorten a pair of trousers, the customer being charged the same price. Because space was at a premium, Jean's office, where she did the business book-keeping, was under the stairs, behind a curtain. As there was no rear garden, Gordon made use of the flat roof space by erecting a shed for Rosemary's bicycle. A garden area was also designed, consisting of pots of flowers and shrubs etc. and was a very colourful area, with panoramic views over the Fox Meadow and the Church as well as a very pleasant vista to the Stowupland heights. In 1959, Rosemary was presented with a younger brother, Richard.

Gordon was soon involved with the town's affairs, holding the posts, at various times, of Chairman of the Urban District Council, Chairman of the Chamber of Trade and also a Trustee of the Stowmarket Town Charities for over forty years. He was also a keen member of the Methodist Church, being Circuit Steward, and helped raise £30,000 for an extension to their building. He helped to set up a Minister's Fraternal and a

(left) 'The Chapel House' next-door to The Kings Head Hotel in Ipswich Street, another 'window' rented by Gordon Ince in the early 1960's.

The cyclist is Mr John Cooper who was the manager of Walkers Store 19 Ipswich Street

GORDON L. INCE LTD.

Complete Men's and Boys' Outfitter

WE ARE STOCKISTS OF:-

Industrial Waterproof Clothing
(Contracts quoted)

Boots and Shoes for the family

Working Clothes

Camping Equipment

Full Range of Fashion clothes for
young men

VISIT OUR MODERN GENTS'
HAIRDRESSING SALOON

Children Always Welcome

Suits to Measure a Speciality

25 IPSWICH STREET
STOWMARKET

Telephone 2664

FABRIC CENTRE

Proprietor : Gordon Ince

For a wonderful selection of

FABRICS for
DRESSMAKING - CURTAINS
LOOSE COVERS - etc.

Dress Patterns in stock
AGENT for Singer & Jones Sewing Machines
Curtains Made to Order

Also, a Fine Range of Hosiery, Handbags,
Haberdashery.

45A IPSWICH STREET STOWMARKET

Ince's shop front at ground level (l.) taken in 1999 prior to a new shop front being fitted in 2000 and (r) the new shop front with a central doorway

Mobile advertising - a modern vehicle advertising Inces parked in the Fox Mews behind the shop

Layman's Fraternal which brought together people from the many different denominations in which two representatives from each church would meet to arrange various ecumenical events for the benefit of the townspeople. He was also involved with the Scout Movement in the town and would produce the programme for each of the Scout Shows, which included selling advertising space in the magazine around the various other trades and businesses in the town. For this work he was awarded the 'Thanks' badge.

In 1967, due to health problems, the business was sold to Mr Ronald (Ron) **Kingsley** of Ipswich. The **Kingsley** family had been connected with the gentlemen's outfitters business for many years prior to this, Ron having been manager at the 'fifty-bob tailor' in Ipswich and his brother John, being manager in the gentlemen's outfitters department of Footman's department store (currently Debenham's). After the Second World War had ended, Ron and John decided to go into business together and founded **Kingsley Bros**., gent's outfitter, in St. Nicholas Street, Ipswich; before long they expanded their

Ince's staff 2002
(l. to r.) Linda Leslie, Julie Smith, Corrine Walls, Derek Moore, Carole Denton & John Kingsley (manager)

business to two further shops in the town. They later chose to move their base away from Ipswich, John preferring Norwich, where he bought **Chadd's** of Bedford Street and Ron, **Ince's** of Stowmarket. Once these new businesses became established, the three Ipswich shops were eventually closed. During this early period, two of Ron's children, John and Linda, helped as Saturday staff. John later went on to become manager at one of the Ipswich shops for a while before taking over **Jonty's** in Tacket Street, Ipswich, being helped by his other sister, Jane.

By 1968 Gordon **Ince's** health improved sufficiently and this prompted him to get back into business, so he set up the Fabric Centre at 45A Ipswich Street, in what had been previously **Newby's** stationers and printers. This venture, selling dress and curtain materials as well as haberdashery, nylon stockings and handbags, was managed by Mr **Crofton-Sleigh**. In 1971 this business too was sold and was taken over by the Sudbury based company of **Winch** and **Blatch** Ltd., managed by Mr Richard **Blatch**. In 1975 Gordon rented the small shop (ex Co-op shoe department) next to the opening through to the Queen's Head Yard (now Capone's) from George **Wilden**, to set Jean up with an antique shop specialising in china and glassware. Jean has a particular interest in, and a great knowledge of, this field. However the shop was then bought from Mr **Wilden** and soon diversified to sell antiques and collectibles from house clearances etc. and ran successfully for ten years until 1985 when the premises were taken over by Cut 'n' Curl hairdressing salon (currently **Chapman's** hairdressers).

Meanwhile, **Ince's** gents' outfitters shop had been running successfully under the management of the **Kingsley** family who maintained the old standards and quality associated with the premises and who also tried new lines to keep pace with fashions and modern trends. Having started to make plans to retire from the business in 1984, Ron brought his son John to Stowmarket to eventually take over the reins. The emphasis is still placed on the traditional core merchandise of hard-wearing work clothes, boots and shoes, sports jackets and country wear and school uniforms, but also diversifying to cover the current fashionable casual wear trends such as fleece jackets and body-warmers, combat trousers, kagoules and trainers etc. They are proud to maintain the reputation of being 'kingsize specialists' in clothes and footwear and try to justify people's expectations of being able to 'get it at **Inces**'.

Gordon **Ince** died in June 1998 aged 82. The shop front has recently undergone major refurbishment work to help set its modern image into the twenty-first century, whilst care has also been taken to preserve the character of the interior of the premises for benefit of future customers and in April 2003, the shop of **'Gordon Ince'** celebrated fifty years of continued service to the community. ❑

GORDON
Ince
clothes for all the family

Lawson's

LADIES' & CHILDREN'S OUTFITTER

Lawson's is a name long associated with ladies' underwear, children's wear and household linens, but the name is purely a trade name, having no connection to any of the families involved with the business. In 1931, despite being in the midst of the great depression, Morley **Bliss** had the courage to open a shop at 22, Ipswich Street. Morley was born on 12th October 1886 at Norwich and his future wife, Maud **Davis**, was born on 16th March 1884 at Drayton, Norfolk. Morley was apprenticed in London and worked for D. H. **Evans** and other large firms. Prior to the outbreak of the First World War, he worked in armament manufacture at Enfield, Middlesex making Royal Enfield rifles; he later joined the LifeGuards and served in the trenches in France. After he was demobbed, he married Maud and they then jointly ran a small hotel at Herne Bay, Kent, where their only child, Betty Kathleen, was born 25th April 1921. The family moved back to Norwich where Morley and Maud were both buyers for **Bond's** department store in Norwich where they both learnt their skills for the drapery trade. As a child in Norwich, Betty was chosen to present a purse of money to Princess Mary, the Princess Royal, at the Jenny **Lind** Hospital.

In 1931, the family moved to Stowmarket and rented the property at 22, Ipswich Street between **Lennard's** shoe shop and the London Meat Company butchers. The premises had formerly been **Fell's** bicycle shop for about six months in 1930, and previously had been a private house with railings in the front. During the Second World War some troops were billeted in these premises and the Army turned the barn at the back into a bathhouse. **Lawson's** originally stocked rugs, carpets and linoleum, as well as what was known as the "Manchester" side of the business, which included household linens of sheets,

Circa 1931, Morley Bliss outside his new shop at 22 Ipswich Street

blankets, towels and tea-towels etc. Betty attended the National School in Milton Road, Stowmarket and during her formative years was a keen Girl Guide. She left school at the age of fourteen to serve an apprenticeship with **Brand's** drapery store in Tacket Street, Ipswich. After learning about the running of the various departments in the store, she returned to the family business. 1938 proved to be a memorable year for the family. It was the year that Morley and Maud moved their business over the road to 31 - 33 Ipswich Street, formerly **Bolton's** shoe shop. Betty met her future husband, Victor (Vic) **Gordon** and another branch was opened opposite the church in the High Street, Needham Market with Betty as manageress. At the time of the move, Morley decided to stop dealing in floor coverings and to concentrate more on the drapery and linens, also to expand their range of ladies' underwear and lingerie items as well as children's clothing. The Needham shop was run along the same lines until Betty signed up for the A.T.S., serving in the Royal Ordnance Corps at Ormskirk, Lancashire, attached to the War Office from 1941, later transferring to Aldershot until the end of the war. Morley had a lucky escape in 1941 when the well-documented bombs fell on the Congregational Chapel. Two of the three shop windows were destroyed in the blast, but the window that he was dressing at the time remained undamaged and he was uninjured. During the dark years of the war, Betty managed to marry Vic **Gordon** during a period when their leaves coincided, strangely, at what was the height of military activity. They were married at Broxbourne in Hertfordshire on D-Day, 6th June 1944 and Betty was demobbed in 1945.

Morley and Maud Bliss

Lawsons Stores LADIES' AND CHILDREN'S OUTFITTERS

(B. K. & V. C. GORDON)

31 & 33 Ipswich Street,
STOWMARKET,
Suffolk.

Telephone:
Stowmarket 2414

A letterhead from the 1950's

Lawson's shop front at 33 Ipswich Street showing damage to a window after being hit by a lorry

Victor Charles **Gordon** was born in Regent Street, Stowmarket, 22nd April 1920, the son of Charles John **Gordon**, a costs clerk at the Guncotton and Cordite works and Alice Sophia (née **Abbott**). They moved to 23, The Crescent, Combs Ford when Vic was one year old. Charles and Alice had another son, Ronald John **Gordon**, who was born 2nd March 1929. Vic was educated at the British School in Childer Road and later the Area School, and was a member of Stowmarket Company of the Boys Brigade for several years, playing in the band and reaching the rank of Staff Sergeant. He left school in 1934 and starting work at the Suffolk Iron Foundry as an office boy. By the time he left to join the services in 1940, he was in the buying department. He joined the Royal Air Force and spent much of his time in the Far East at places including India, Malaya and Singapore, leaving from Java before being demobbed in April 1946. His mother, Alice, had died in January 1941 shortly after he entered the services, and his father, Charles, died in the same month as his demobilisation.

After the end of the war, Betty and Vic lived above the shop at 33, Ipswich Street, a Georgian building which had formerly been a doctor's house. Betty worked in her parents' shop, whilst Vic went back to the Suffolk Iron Foundry where he worked as a Mature Controller until 1948. On 27th. October that year, their daughter, Jane Elizabeth, was born above the shop. Vic decided to leave his job at the Suffolk Iron Foundry so that he could help his in-laws in the family business. As the Congregational Chapel in Ipswich Street had been destroyed in 1941, this meant all church services for some time had to be held at the Regal Cinema. It was during this time that Jane was christened at the cinema by the Reverend Eric J. **Weir**. In 1951, Maud and Morley **Bliss** retired to Felixstowe and Betty and Vic took over the business in their own names, although

Morley Bliss with his daughter Betty and her husband Vic Gordon in their garden off Church Walk (currently Hicks' car park)

they retained the trade name of **Lawson's**. In the early hours of Valentines Day, 14th February 1962, after a heavy fall of snow, a lorry skidded and crashed into the shop sending a shower of broken glass into the display of baby clothes, the entire stock having to be destroyed. Anglia Television reported the incident with their cameras displaying the damage on the local news bulletin. Morley enjoyed thirteen years of retirement at Felixstowe until his death on 9th November 1964 aged seventy-eight. Following her husband's death, Maud moved back to Stowmarket and lived once more over the shop in rooms converted by Vic for her comfort, until her death on 18th April 1967 aged eighty-three.

Morley and Maud Bliss at Felixstowe after their retirement

The shop building is quite an old structure and has cellars that were used for storage. The garden at the rear of the premises was situated on the opposite side of Church Walk and used to be part of a group of small houses known as Cabbage Square. Vic had the site cleared of the remains of the buildings and turned it into a secluded town garden; this was later sold to Brian **Hicks** and is currently the private car park for **Hicks'** vans and customers.

Telephone: 2414

31-33 IPSWICH STREET,
STOWMARKET, SUFFOLK.

........................19....

M..

Dr. to **LAWSON'S STORES**

(B. K. & V. C. GORDON)

Ladies' and Children's Outfitters

LAWSON'S

For Dependable Quality

—□—

Drapery, Ladies' and Children's
Hosiery, Underwear, Overalls,
Frocks, Baby Linen, Household
Linens, Rugs, Carpets, etc., etc.

—□—

IPSWICH STREET,
STOWMARKET

LAWSONS

(B. K. & V. C. GORDON)

LADIES and CHILDRENS WEAR

SPECIALIST IN BABY LINEN

31 & 33 IPSWICH STREET
STOWMARKET

Telephone 2414

Vic was for some time an active member of the Chamber of Trade, serving a term as President from 1961 - 1963 and was involved with discussions with the Ministry of Transport about the need for a Relief Road for the town. This was due in part to the regular traffic jams through the town as well as the sunblind on the shop (needed to protect the delicate fabrics in a south facing window from fading) that were often being damaged by the large lorries that used to come through the narrow street. Vic was a member of the Stowmarket Operatic and Dramatic Society appearing in many plays and musicals such as 'Maria **Marten**', 'This Happy Breed' and 'Sailor Beware'. Before performances were held at the Regal Theatre they used to be staged in St Peter's Church Hall, Milton Road and it was the normal procedure to hire the three hundred chairs required for each play from **Cole** & Son (Furnishers) Ltd.

Betty and Vic Gordon

Working in a shop that sold ladies' underwear produced the occasional humorous moment. Vic recalled one Saturday a lady came in to purchase a brassiere, the size and type were given and the item was duly parcelled up. The following Monday, a young boy came into the shop who could barely see over the counter upon which he slid the parcel. Vic read the attached note that said, "the brassiere that I bought on Saturday was not suitable, please could you exchange it for a pair of pillowcases". He also remembers being asked to exchange a nightdress that clashed with the buyer's bedroom wallpaper. Another point of interest was the use of tokens given as change. These were stamped with the '**Lawson**' name and had values ranging from 1d (less than ½ p) to 6d (2½p) and were used in place of coin of the realm to encourage further sales (similar ideas were used in other shops across the country).

Betty and Vic's daughter, Jane, had been educated at Hillcroft School and Stowmarket Grammar school before joining the staff at **Corder's** of Ipswich to learn the drapery business. She later joined her parents in the busy Stowmarket shop that also sold curtain and dress fabrics, knitting wool and haberdashery. They announced their retirement on 22nd November 1973, bringing about its closure after forty-two years of trading. The **Gordon** family then moved to a house in Finborough Road where they enjoyed several years retirement until 1986 when Betty fell ill and required special care, which Vic provided until her death in 1993.

Berwick's Estate Agents, East Anglian Daily Times/Evening Star Office and the Woolwich Building Society currently occupy the premises. ❑

LAWSONS

BABY, CHILDREN'S AND LADIES' WEAR
31/33 IPSWICH STREET, STOWMARKET

Closing Down Sale

Having sold our property, this business will close shortly. We wish to thank our many customers for their patronage over the past 42 years.

BUY YOUR CHRISTMAS
GIFTS NOW AND SAVE

The Galleon Café

W H AND W B MAYCOCK

There will no doubt be many people from Stowmarket and surrounding villages who will have fond memories of popping into the 'Galleon', perhaps for breakfast or at least a cup of tea before going to work or catching a bus. Many others will remember it as an evening meeting place to socialize over a soft drink and listen to the latest pop-songs on the juke-box.

The 'Galleon' at 16 Market Place had been a butchers shop in the early part of the century, owned by Herbert **Arnold**. It was then run as a wet-fish shop by George **Wilden** during the 'thirties. When George **Wilden** relocated his business to 12 Market Place (where it became **Bloomfield's**), the premises at 16 Market Place became the 'Mulberry Tree Club' for servicemen throughout the war years of the 1940's. It became the 'Galleon' (the family know of no significance or reason for the name) in 1947 when it was bought by William Henry (Bill) **Maycock** and his wife Isabella (Bella) née **Brown**.

William Henry **Maycock** was born January 22nd 1906, the youngest of five children of Tom **Maycock** and Mary Ann **Fidler** of Buxton, Derbyshire. The other children were: Mary Emma, born 1900; Tom, born 1901; Ada, born 1903 and Winifred, born 1904. By 1925 Bill had married Bella, who was born in Manchester in July 1907 and moved to Suffolk where their first child, William Basil (Bill junior) **Maycock** was born at Felixstowe on December 14th 1925. Ten years later the family had moved to Holbrook where their daughter, Barbara, was born on October 8th 1935. During this period Bill and

Bill and Bella Maycock with Bill junior

Bella kept the Post Office at Holbrook and Bill also drove for the Royal Hospital School. At the start of the War in 1939 Bill joined the Royal Navy and was followed in 1943 by Bill junior when he reached the age of eighteen. Shortly after leaving the Services, the family moved to Stowmarket and was able to acquire the 'Mulberry Tree' servicemen's club which had stood empty for some while and in February 1947 founded the 'Galleon'. The original set-up in this three-storey building had a first floor restaurant serving hot meals, as well as a café snack bar on the ground floor, whilst the family lived on the top floor. Within a year of opening, it became the daily routine of a young filing clerk to stop there for a cup of tea before catching the bus to Finborough where she worked for Eastern Electricity. Shelagh **High** was born in 1928 the daughter of William **High** and Lily (née **James**). Shelagh's parents had farmed at Hoxne but in 1946 had moved to Bridge Farm, Old Newton. It was from here that Shelagh would cycle into town and leave her bike in the yard behind **Codd's** bicycle shop in Station Road, then walk to the Market Place where she attracted the attention of Bill **Maycock** junior. The following paragraph from the 'Finborough Review', an Eastern Electricity Board staff magazine, dated December 1949, reads: "Although the first impressions gathered was that our Miss S. G. **High**, of the Filing and Postal Section, was a member of the party who welcomed the Viking ship 'Hugon', we are now in a

Bill and Bella in the early 1950's

Proprietors: Maycock & Son **Telephone: Stowmarket 437**

16-18 Market Place
Stowmarket
Suffolk

The Galleon Cafe

HADKINS' PURE ICES

Always
Something Tasty
at the GALLEON

The Galleon advertised in the town's 1953 Coronation celebration pamphlet

position to verify that the 'Galleon' which she has been frequenting is land-based, and as an outcome of these visits we are delighted to announce that a betrothal ensued which terminated in the ringing of the church bells at Stowmarket on 29th October, when she walked up the aisle to take the hand of Mr W. **Maycock**. Before saying goodbye to her friends, Miss **High** was presented with a cheque by Mr W. **Smith**, on behalf of the department."

An early photograph of the 'Galleon' showing the door to the upstairs café & the giant ice-cream cone above the shop sign

Shelagh quickly realised that she enjoyed this kind of work, which involved meeting people and being in the centre of town, the 'Galleon' very soon became a focal point for many people. The hours were long, as they were open from 5:45am to 10:00pm seven days per week; Sunday opening hours were 9:00am to 10:00pm and they were only closed on Christmas Day. The main business consisted of providing sandwiches, snacks, cakes, tea, coffee and soft drinks etc. In the early days Bill, Bella and Bill junior baked their own cakes and fancies. The sandwiches were made with fresh bread delivered daily from **Palmer's** (Haughley) bakery. However, after they became established, the cake-baking became the domain of Mr Ernest **Hedley** who was to stay several years before setting off on his own and opening up his own business near St Matthew's Baths in Ipswich. Shelagh describes the early days as being very hectic, as lorries containing gangs of Eastern Electricity workers would congregate in the Market Place and call in for an early morning cup of tea, buy sandwiches and cakes etc to eat throughout the day. They were able to buy their favourite brands of cigarettes and tobacco and other such daily requirements from the 'Galleon' as well. She also recalls that for the two hours up to 8:00am the premises seemed to be bursting

The motor-cycle ice-cream cart that was used in the 1950's, here seen at the Needham Market Carnival

at the seams with people arriving from the buses who would call in before going to work at the foundry, as well as other shops, offices and businesses in the town. The morning would see a steady stream of shoppers including housewives with young children. Lunchtime would be busy with the people from the shops, offices and factories making the 'Galleon' their main port of call for their refreshments. The afternoon session was similar to the morning. There would be another flurry of activity as the shops and offices closed at either 5:00pm or 5:30pm. Then from 6:30pm onwards the 'Galleon' staff would gear up for the youngsters to congregate for the evening. Alongside Bill and Bella, Bill junior and Shelagh, there were thirteen part time staff including Christine **Smith**, later to become Mrs **White** of **White's** Newsagents and Stores, Wolsey Road. Christine remembers each day seeming to have "a different smell", especially Market Days when farmers and their stockmen called into the 'Galleon' bringing in on their boots the natural by-product found on the floors of livestock markets. Christine also emphasised the relaxed and friendly atmosphere both for working in and when off duty and how customers would not be pressed to buy more than one drink even when sitting and socialising and listening to the Juke Box for many hours. This made the 'Galleon' a favourite meeting place for courting couples and was where Christine would meet her future husband Arthur ('Chalkie') **White** when he was on leave from RAF Wattisham. Bill and Bella would serve in the café from 6:00am till

The Market Place showing the 'Galleon' in between the Ministry of National Insurance office and the International Stores, circa 1949

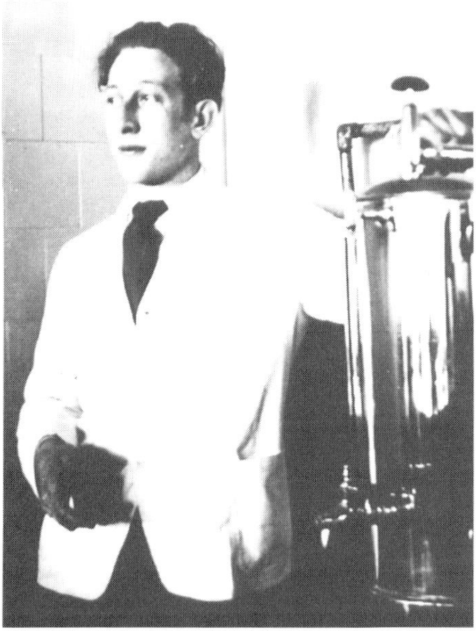

Bill Maycock junior beside his tea urn

8:00am, then bake their cakes. Shelagh and one or two of her part time staff would do the 8:00am till 4:00pm session, Bill junior did 4:00pm till 7:00pm when Mrs Winifred **Webb** would take over till 10:00pm.

Bill junior and Shelagh's first child, George William, was born December 15th 1952 and in January 1953 it was found necessary to increase the cost of a cup of tea from 2½d (1p) to 3d (1½p) at which the comment was made 'I s'pose this means you're gonna put the price of tea up every time you have a babe!' However, this seems not to have been the case as there was no price increase or comments made when Richard John was born on October 16th 1954. Although George and Richard were never to have any part in the ownership of the business, as soon as they were considered old enough they were expected to help at times, to earn their

Christine Smith (l.) with Shelagh in front of the cigarette shelf, with brands such as Navy Cut, Gold Leaf and Player's Weights. Ovaltine mugs can also be seen

Shelagh Maycock (l.) with a selection of pies in the foreground

pocket-money. This involved them collecting up the dirty crockery on large trolleys and taking them out to the kitchen where everything had to be washed by hand, usually by Mrs **Thorpe** (weekdays) and Mrs **Newstead** (Sundays).

Throughout the 1950's the 'Galleon' was able to provide ice-cream to the town's population as well. The ice-cream was made and supplied by Bill senior's sister, Mary Emma, (1900-1973) who was married to Algernon Ernest **Hadkins** and lived at Felixstowe. Mary was also helped by her other brother, Tom (1901-1975). The ice-cream was dispensed from a small window, which opened onto the street and was situated beside the main cafeteria window. They also ran an ice-cream van that had rounds covering the town and local villages. **Hadkins** ices could be bought locally from a roundsman on a motorcycle combination. Shelagh remembers that when the main street was full of people waiting for the arrival of the carnival procession, the motorcycle ice-cream vendor slowly drove along the street waving regally to the crowds before the floats began to appear.

When Bill and Bella retired they moved to 1, Windermere Road, but unfortunately Bella died in January 1971, aged sixty-four. However, for a while Bill would help out as relief when other shop staff were on holiday, but this arrangement did not last for

A surving 'Galleon' cup and saucer

The Market Place in the 1970's when it was Theobald's 'Galleon' Grill

too long as by December 1972 Bill junior had decided to sell the business, although Shelagh had tried to persuade him to carry on. The business was sold to **Theobald's** and became known as **Theobald's** 'Galleon' Grill. Bill and Shelagh then planned to sell their bungalow, 'Spinnakers' at Elmswell and move to Spain but sadly this was not to be, as, a few months later in April 1973, Bill junior died aged only forty-seven. Bill senior died in 1982 aged seventy-six. By the late 1970's the building became the property of the Abbey National Building Society, with whom it remains to this day.

Shelagh moved from Elmswell and lived for several years at 32 St Peter's Road and then moved to 65 Stowmarket Road, Needham Market. Although past normal retirement age, Shelagh, who says she still loves meeting people, continues to work serving customers at **Palmer's** (Haughley) bakery, which not only involves working part-time in the Station Road branch, but also at their other branches in Stanton and Woolpit etc. ❑

A close-up of Theobald's 'Galleon' Grill

J M Mayhew & Son

BAKERS & CONFECTIONERS

James Marsden **Mayhew** was born in Woodbridge, 25th April 1834, son of James Riches **Mayhew** and his wife Emma (née **Smith**). He was baptised at St. Mary's Church, Woodbridge on the 23rd May 1834. His father had continued in the family's long-standing bakery trade by running his own established bakery business. The business was started by James Marsden's grandfather, also James, of Great Waldingfield, in the Market Hill in Woodbridge, around 1810. When James (grandfather) died in 1823, his widow Sarah took over, followed by her son James Riches **Mayhew** and the business was listed in the White's Directory of 1844, as baker, flour dealer and confectioner. The business was still listed again in the 1855 directory but does not appear in the 1875 lists as he retired a few years earlier.

James Marsden **Mayhew** had moved to Pleasant Row, Stowmarket by 1861, so that by the time of his marriage to Eliza **Codd** on 27th October 1863, both the bride and groom were described as being resident in Stowmarket. On the wedding certificate he is also described as a baker; Eliza was the daughter of Eldred **Codd**, a storekeeper and sister to Keziah **Codd** (named as **Lord** in error in 'Serving You Through The Years' Book I) who married William J. **Palmer** (Palmer's Bakery). Their first two children, James Riches **Mayhew**, 1865, and Eldred Codd **Mayhew**, 1866, were born at Regent Terrace; the next four children George Marsden, 1867, Caroline Maud (Cissy), 1868, Annie Eliza, 1870 and Florence Emma, 1872 were all born in Bury Street. In a **Morris** and Company's commercial directory and gazetteer for 1868, J. M. **Mayhew** is listed as a baker and confectioner at Bury Street and Market Place. By the time that Florence Emma **Mayhew** died at the age of fifteen months, the family had moved to premises in Ipswich Street. William Simon, 1873, Fanny Isabel, 1875 and Frederick Pearson, 1876, were all born at the Ipswich Street bakery. In the 1881 census the family is shown as living in Ipswich Street. The list shows James senior, forty-three, confectioner, Eliza his wife aged thirty-nine, James junior, sixteen, a Post Office clerk and Eldred, fifteen, a chemist's assistant (for the **Prentice** Brothers), George, thirteen, Caroline, twelve, William, seven, are scholars with

James Marsden Mayhew

James Marsden Mayhew (right) outside his shop with his 15 year-old son William, standing in the doorway.

The Mayhew family: (l. to r.) Fred (lying on ground), Eliza (seated hand on chin), Eldred (seated), Caroline (with bicycle), William Simon (seated hand on chin), George (wearing hat), Fanny (seated) and Eliza Lillian (on lounger)

The Mayhew brothers:
Eldred (standing) with Fred (left) and William Simon (right)

Fanny, six and Frederick, four and also twenty year old Harry J. **Lyas** from Buxhall, a servant employed as a baker. By the time of the 1891 census both James senior and James junior still have the same occupations, but by this time Eldred is listed as a baker and confectioner, Caroline a schoolmistress, Annie a confectioner's assistant, William a grocer's assistant, Fanny a scholar and Frederick a Post Office messenger.

James Marsden **Mayhew**, Master Baker, who had delivered bread on his hand cart for Stow Lodge when it was the Workhouse, died at the Ipswich Street shop on 21st December 1895, aged sixty-one. His wife Eliza and sons Eldred and William continued the business with other members of the family, assisting in the general running of the bakery, shop and tearoom. After the death of her husband, Eliza moved to 11, Tavern Street and gave the property the name of 'Marsden House' by which it is still known today. Due to legislation passed in the early 1900's, all premises had to be numbered and so **Mayhew's** bakery became number eleven Ipswich Street (the site now occupied by QD Stores). William Simon **Mayhew**, baker/ confectioner, aged twenty-

A Mayhew delivery boy

Eldred Codd Mayhew

nine, married Eliza Lilian, the twenty-two year old daughter of the late George **Flowers**, at Stowmarket 12th August 1902. Frederick Pearson **Mayhew**, confectioner's assistant, died at 11, Ipswich Street 4th November 1915, aged thirty-nine.

By the end of the First World War, **Mayhew's** had been trading for nearly fifty years; their reputation had grown so fast that extra staff were taken on. One of these was Violet **Woods**, whose father was farm bailiff at Badley Hall. In 1924, upon leaving school aged fourteen, her younger sister Murial (Millie) joined Violet, who was by this time a confectioner. So that she could start work at seven o' clock each morning, Millie took lodgings (bed only) with Miss **Barnard** in Cardinal's Road at two shillings per week. Meals were generously provided for the staff at the shop by the **Mayhew** brothers, consisting of a breakfast at nine o'clock, a cooked midday meal (just for some of the staff after the customers had finished their lunch)

Mayhew's shop front displaying their wares circa 1920

Murial (Millie) Woods

and a cup of tea and a cake for their tea before going home. Millie began learning about the various aspects of bakery and confectionery whilst doing some of the more menial tasks such as washing and cleaning pans, trays and work surfaces, her weekly wage being four shillings and sixpence (4/6d) (23p). After four years, when Violet left to get married and moved to Ipswich, Millie saw her chance and asked for her sister's job. She was given a month's trial in the confectionery side of the business, doing sugarcraft and making fancy cakes etc. She excelled and was able to maintain the high standard that had given the company such a good reputation. She was told that if she could keep the standard going, the job was hers. After her post was confirmed, her wages were increased by two shillings and sixpence (2/6d) (12 ½p) to seven shillings (7/-) (35p) per week. Her apprenticeship was served under Mr Sidney **Smith**, a Master confectioner, where she learned to make glacés, petit fours, Genoese and gateaux. Millie remembers that of the **Mayhew** brothers, William (Mr Willie) was the baker and Eldred was the manager of the whole business. Eldred's confectionery was marvelled at by Millie who insists that his marzipan roses and bowls of fruit could easily be mistaken for the real thing. **Mayhew's** catered for functions at various places, including the Felix Hotel in Felixstowe, where their delicate creations had to be carefully transported by car. Millie explained that the

Inside the bakery
(l. to r.) Mr Bridgeman, Violet Woods, Arthur Hedge, William S. (Mr Willie) Mayhew, Louis Robinson, Bertie Green & Sidney Smith

One of the many elaborate Mayhew's wedding cakes

hump-back bridge over the river at Claydon would cause them problems if the driver of the open top Lancia tried to take it too fast. The Felixstowe trip was to provide fancies, thirty-six dozen at a time, for the annual tennis tournaments. The team of helpers employed on these trips would usually consist of Mr Willie, Mr Sidney **Smith**, Mr Bertie **Green**, Millie **Woods** and Elizabeth (Lizzie) **Allum** (Mr **Bridgeman** helped in later years). Other outlets where **Mayhew's** fancies were sold included **Jaclyn's** of Colchester, **Hewitt's** of Ipswich, **Parr's** of Needham Market, **Aldridge and Bryant** at Woodbridge and Framlingham.

Mayhew's were also renowned for their quality bread products, baked in the four large coke-fired ovens along the rear wall at the back of the premises, once known as Catt's Lane (as detailed in property deeds dated 1732). The bread dough was mixed in **Hobart** machines and set in provers immediately beneath the ovens. One pound and three pound loaves in white, Hovis and wholemeal, made up the bulk of the daily requirements, together with twists, plaits and cottage loaves as well as round, long and finger rolls. They were also known for their savoury products, such as hand-raised pork pies, beef patties and sausage rolls, the latter being rolled in one long strip along the length of the table before being cut into individual portions. Naturally **Mayhew's** wares were served in their own tea-rooms; customers could order a pot of tea with a roll and butter or a doughnut, ham sandwiches, scones and butter and their famed fancies.

Every year, Maundy Thursday proved to be a busy time for the entire staff, as seven thousand hot-cross buns were produced in addition to the normal daily routine work; staff would start at 4:00am to deal with these extra duties. At Easter time, Easter cakes, hand-made chocolate eggs and Simnel cakes were a speciality as well as sponge nests decorated with cream, stranded brown coconut for twigs, tiny meringue eggs and yellow chicks. An annual tradition at that time of year was to make a huge chocolate egg, from which appeared marzipan pigs all set on green shredded marzipan grass. This would then presented to the local children's home by Mr Laurence Bernard **Lister** of **Woodward** and **Woodward** auctioneers and estate agents. Christmas was also a busy time when mince pies, chocolate tree-stumps, chocolate logs and Christmas cakes were made and sold,

Staff relaxing at the rear of Mayhew's in the 1950's
(l. to r.) Rita Mayhew, Shirley Deal, Heather Welham and Ann Copeland

STOWMARKET SHOPPING WEEK, June 11th—20th, 1931

Wedding Cakes -

OF OUTSTANDING QUALITY

We have a reputation of 60 years for these Cakes and are privileged to send them to all parts of the Country

The ingredients are carefully chosen and every Cake is beautifully matured, richly Almond Iced and completed in first style

PRICES FROM 10/6 TO £12 12. 0.

WEDDING CAKE ON CUT - 3/- per lb.

Wedding Cards Confetti Wedding Cake Boxes

Receptions carefully and artistically catered for in every detail - - - -

See Windows and ask for Booklet "Wedding Etequette"

J. M. MAYHEW & SON

Confectioners - **Stowmarket**

'PHONE 27.

Winners of 40 Gold and Silver Medals—London Exhibition

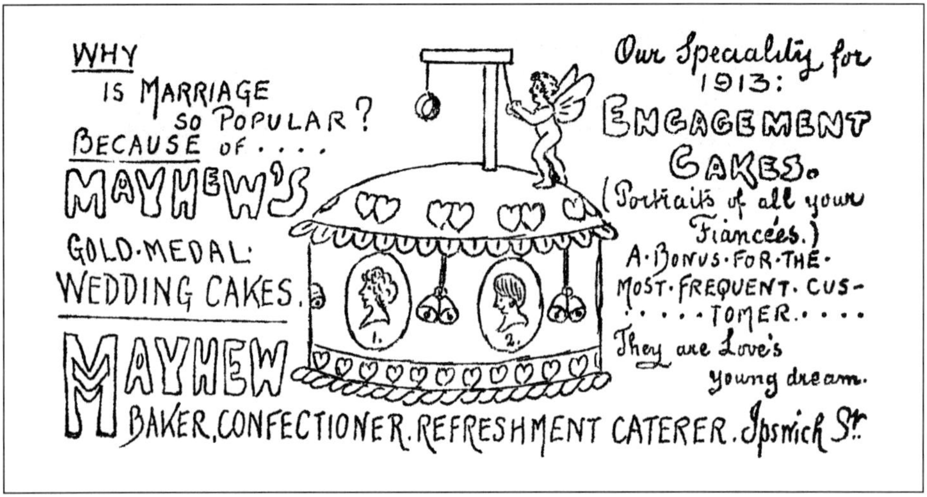

Mayhew's advertisements in the 1913 and 1914 editions of the
Stow Dramatic Intelligencer and Trade Boomster

with staff working until 11:00 p.m. on some evenings running up to the holiday period. It is well remembered that the **Mayhew** family organised parties for their staff and partners after Christmas each year, at either the Oddfellows' Hall or the Constitutional Hall. These functions had music provided by a local band and refreshments that the staff had prepared themselves. They were an annual event that started after the First World War and continued until the shop closed at the end of the 1950's. **Mayhew's** other main operations were catering for wedding receptions, providing sandwich buffets and wedding cakes, Masonic functions in the Church Hall and teas in the marquee for the judges and committee of the annual Hill House flower show. William Simon (Mr Willie) died at Stowmarket 12th February 1928.

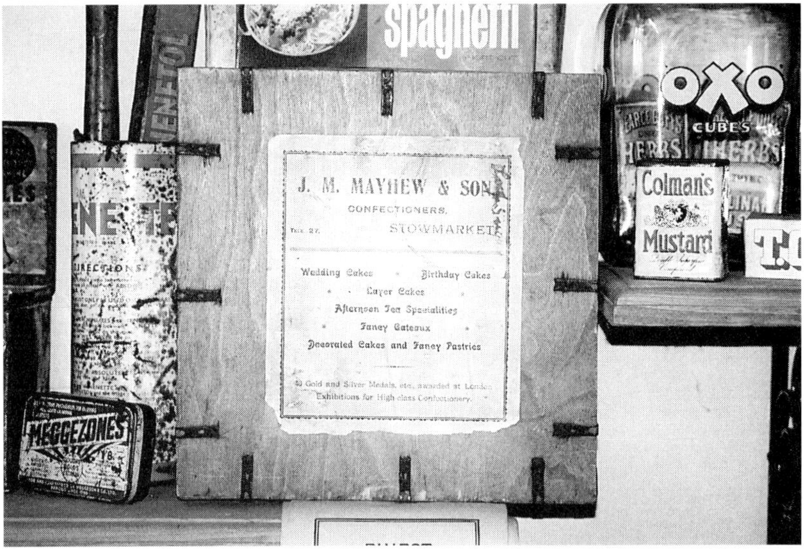

Part of a display at a museum at Brook Farm, Buxhall showing a wooden box for delivering Mayhew's cakes arranged with other tins and jars of the 1930's period ***(By kind permission of Mr & Mrs P. Jordon)***

During the Second World War, evacuees could be seen queuing outside the Ipswich Street shop for their ration of bread and cake. At the end of the war Eldred decided to retire. Due to early deaths and family moving away from the area, Eldred, a bachelor, realised that he was left with no family to inherit the business. He tried to persuade his brother William's two children to become interested but neither Leslie (at **Fison's**) nor Doris (at **Stannard's**) was willing to join their uncle in the family business, so he sold the business to Sydney **Smith** the head confectioner. Sydney was only to hold the reins for three years as in 1948 he died suddenly at the age of fifty-six; the business was then passed to his wife, but in the early 1950's she sold the concern on to Mr **Cooper** who also owned **Westgate's** of Felixstowe. John **Cooper**, son of the owner, managed the Stowmarket business; another son, Peter managed the Felixstowe shop.

Rita **Gibbons** (née **Mayhew**, not related) has fond memories of her time in the bakery, where in 1952 she began working as a general assistant. Her earlier duties included washing up and cleaning working surfaces etc. She then progressed to helping to split and fill eclairs as

A view of Mayhew's shop which was probably taken shortly before closure i.e. in the late 1950's

well as injecting doughnuts with jam from a syringe. Vast quantities of ingredients were ordered from various suppliers: these included **Cranfield's** for flour, **Renshaw's** for marzipan and cake decorations, **Chivers** for jam and mincemeat (purchased in seven and fourteen pound tins) and **Burton** Son and **Saunders** for sugars, fats, dried fruit (which came in wooden tea chests), casks of port and rum in wicker baskets (for wedding cakes), rice flour and rice paper etc. Farm eggs were purchased by the gallon from **Wilden's** fishshop in the town (a gallon equalling 360 eggs).

Eldred Codd **Mayhew** died at Marsden House, 11, Tavern Street, 9th August 1952 aged eighty-six.

The shop was closed in 1959 and the premises were subsequently demolished in the early 1960's along with neighbouring properties and redeveloped and occupied by a new Key Markets supermarket store. ❑

Stramit International Ltd
(Mosesson Family)

CONSTRUCTION MATERIAL MANUFACTURERS

The Tomo Industrial Estate off the Creeting Road is known by most people in the town, but few people know that 'Tomo' comes from the first two letters of each of Torsten **Mosesson's** names. It also means 'friend' in the Japanese language.

The **Mosesson** (the name means 'son of Moses') family came from the small town of Lindesberg in central Sweden, which is between Oslo and Stockholm and had long been associated with the timber trade. Torsten **Mosesson** was born in 1906, one of the six children of John and Selma, also **Mosesson**. The other children were: Saga born 1904, sadly died aged eighteen months, Runa born 1908, Birgitta born 1910, Stig born 1912 and Daga born 1914. When he was aged twenty in 1925, Torsten left Sweden for Peru in South America to set up an agency, based in Lima, selling Swedish products ranging from ball-bearings to sewing machines etc. During the ten years on that continent he also spent some time in Columbia and Argentina before returning to Sweden to take over the family business. As he passed through England he saw an opportunity to introduce more advanced Swedish window and door manufacturing methods. By chance he met Brita **Michelson** in London in 1935, who also came from Lindesberg and they returned to Sweden to get married in 1936. In the same year he came back to England to set up the joinery company 'Linden Doors' (derived from the name of their home village and

Mosesson family photograph taken at Lindesberg, Sweden 1930, seated (l. to r.) Daga, Selma (mother), John (father) and Runa standing (l. to r.) Birgitta, Stig and Torsten

Torsten Mosesson at his marriage to Brita Michelson in Lindesberg 1936. She was a Scout leader and is giving the Scout salute to some of her attendants

referring to the Linden tree) and was one of the first tenants on the Slough Trading Estate. Joinery and components were imported and assembled on the estate. Two years later, Torsten purchased another site and developed a sawmill at West Drayton on the Grand Union Canal; this was a Packet Boat dock where rough-cut timber was brought in barges from the Thames and the wood was machined at the sawmill to produce windows and doors. Torsten and Brita had their first child, John, in July 1938. The country was already preparing for the forthcoming war and the company was called into the War Effort by the Ministry of Works, using their facilities and local timber. Torsten sent Brita and John back to Sweden for safety as the war loomed, but they returned in 1939 when the family moved to Beaconsfield, a village on the A40 road half way between London and Oxford and within easy reach of the West Drayton Works.

During the war period, Torsten and Brita had three more sons: Michael, born 1942, Anders, born 1944 and Lars, born 1946. Meanwhile, as the war drew to a close, Torsten, who had been given the rank of Colonel in the British Army, was asked by the British Government to travel across Europe in search of new types of building materials to help rebuild houses and factories that had been damaged during the hostilities. Torsten had the vision that timber was a finite product and as the war had used up many natural resources, it was even more important to find new methods for the reconstruction programme. Ironically, after having looked around Europe, the answer was to be found in his native Sweden, where an experiment to compress and consolidate wheat straw into panels was being carried out. This became known as the *Stramit* method, the name being derived from 'stramen', being the Latin word for straw. Although it had been used for ten years in Sweden, the process still needed some refinement. Torsten saw its potential and in 1945, the Tomo Trading Company Limited acquired from Sweden the rights to the Stramit method and patents of manufacturing a building slab from compressed straw. Now a suitable site had to be found close to a straw producing area. Suffolk was suggested as a likely venue by Basil **Arent** of Oulton Broad and in 1946 when the Great Eastern Works in Creeting

Torsten's father John with his brothers and sister on their visit to England in 1952 (l. to r.) Ester (an educationist who has a college named after her in Gottenburgh), Gustav (became leader of the Liberal Party in the Swedish Parliament), Petrus (became Swedish Consul in France), John (owned window and door factory and was mayor of Lindesberg)

Torsten, Chairman with H.E. the Swedish Ambassador Gunnar Hägglöt, Honorary President who had opened the Coronation Barn in 1958

Road, Stowmarket (used for the munitions industry during the war) became vacant, the fourteen and a half acre site with its two hundred and fifty thousand square feet of buildings was seen as a good choice. Its proximity to rail (the site had its own sidings) and road links were very important and so the first Stramit machine was installed there in 1946; an arrangement lasting for three years was made with Messrs. Bowaters to supply the paper liner and act as distributors for the finished product. The new venture was registered as Stramit Boards Limited on 24th December the same year and after some early 'teething troubles' connected with power cuts etc., the first delivery of Stramit board finally appeared in March 1947.

For the first ten years the plant at Stowmarket continued to grow, consisting of seven machines of Swedish origin (capable of working around the clock), a system of mechanical handling and cleaning of the straw and equipment to give the standard slabs special sizes and finishes. There was an engineering shop to deal with maintenance

The arches erected in The Mall for the 1953 Coronation

The arches arriving by road at Stowmarket

The construction of the 'Coronation Barn'

The team that clad the Coronation Barn celebrating the 'topping out ceremony' fitting the last panel on March 9th 1957 (l to r) : David Cracknell, Bert Brown, Phil Waspe, Jack Alexander, George (Old Sacker) Robinson, Old Josh, Bert (Lob) Robinson and Percy Gooding

The completed barn

Aerial view of the Tomo site with the Coronation Barn (top centre)

and development work and a laboratory for production control and development studies. Directly after the war, a shortage of mainstay building materials meant that short-term stop-gap measures had to be utilised in the post-war building boom. Stramit worked hard not to be included in this category through extensive research and development and achieved a recognised quality standard, BRITISH STANDARD 4046. Two of the main uses for Stramit boards were for flat roofing and partitioning used primarily in housing and latterly in school buildings, as a direct result of the Education Act of 1943, which proved to be an immense task. Stramit's success showed in the fact that there was hardly a county in England that had not used their product. At the height of the process in Stowmarket, every day, one hundred and fifty straw-laden lorries would have to pass through the town, cross the Stowupland Road level crossing and head along the Creeting Road to the site to keep the machines running. There are eleven parts to the process of making Stramit boards. Firstly the straw bales are loaded onto an automatic feed system, then a special bale opening system opens the bales without damaging them. A separator then removes stones and other impurities, any remaining grain being separated and sold. A hopper aligns the cleaned straw and feeds it into the slab-forming section at the correct rate and special additives are added at this point. The compacted board core is extruded through a heated tunnel with a series of extrusion beds. The consolidation of straw core is achieved by the technology of heating and compression without any added resin binders. A liner is then bonded to the core surfaces during further extrusion (re-cycled paper is often used but other optional linings can be added at this stage). The weight and density are monitored during the cooling and curing stage. The board then passes through the saw unit where the cutting to the required length is done on a moving rig to allow a continuous production process. Each slab is then 'endsealed' where the cut ends of the panels are sealed with endpapers, applied by heat and pressure. The panels are then quality checked and moved to storage.

The front cover of the first Newsletter produced by the Tomo company in 1959 showing aerial views of both the Slough and Stowmarket sites as well as some of their products

In 1953 Stramit boards were used for the Westminster Abbey annex, which was erected especially for the Coronation of Queen Elizabeth II. It would be reasonable to assume that whilst in London during this period, Torsten admired the Coronation arches that had been erected along The Mall. In 1955 he had the idea for using the arches as main supports for a proposed new building at Stowmarket and negotiations took place with the Ministry of Works for their purchase, being successfully completed by May the same year. After some modifications, the arches were transported by rail to Stowmarket where they were hoisted onto previously prepared plinths by a fifteen ton crane with a forty foot jib. The building measured 105 feet long x 130 feet wide x 60 feet high to the apex and was capable of storing two thousand tons of baled straw. The concrete plinths required to carry the weight of the structure were one metre square each and bevelled, although they had to be made to different heights to accommodate the differing lengths of the steel arches. The Ipswich firm of **Cocksedge's** were the main contractors for the steel erection, but Stramit staff were used to clad the building with Stramit boards. This process involved the boards being hauled into place by a tractor pulling each panel up from the opposite side of the building until its correct position had been reached and then held in place by special clips. Felt tiles were then added to the boards being stuck down with pitch with a third of their area used as overlap. This building was made more prominent from the Creeting Road end of town by having 'Stramit' painted in large letters along its side; however, its life span was very short as in the autumn of 1961 a fire was begun by sparks from a conveyor igniting straw dust in an underground tunnel. This was a major set-back but a new purpose-built hangar-style building was soon erected on the same site. About this time, however, lack of space at the Stowmarket site forced Torsten to negotiate for a one hundred acre site at Eye on part of the old wartime

Straw lorries queued up in the access road off Creeting Road leading to the Tomo site

An advertising display circa 1950, designed by art teacher Miss Rosemary Croft, who had been suggested to Jack Gascoine for her artwork when he was planning an exhibition stand. Rosemary eventually became Mrs Gascoine

FROM THE FARMS OF EAST ANGLIA ALONE EIGHTY TO ONE HUNDRED TONS OF SELECTED STRAW ARE USED EVERY WEEK IN THE MANUFACTURE OF STRAMIT BOARDS.

THE STRAW MUST BE LONG CLEAN AND DRY PREFERABLY WHEAT STRAW THOUGH RYE AND BARLEY ARE USED

STRAMIT BOARDS

LTD

THE STOWMARKET FACTORY

CREETING ROAD

- EMPLOYS FORTY LOCAL MEN AND WOMEN
- PRODUCES OVER A THOUSDAND BOARDS EACH WEEK
- HAS TRANSFORMED A DERELICT SITE INTO A THRIVING CENTRE OF INDUSTRY

STRAMIT BOARDS

- ARE MADE EXCLUSIVELY FOR BUILDING
- ARE MANUFACTURED IN TWELVE COUNTRIES
- ARE PERMANENT EASY TO USE AND ECONOMICAL
- PROVIDE INSULATION EQUAL TO THAT OF SOLID BRICK
- ARE RESISTANT TO WIND & FIRE

THOUSANDS OF LONDON HOMES, AND NEW HOUSES IN STOWMARKET, HAVE WATER TANKS INSULATED BY MEANS OF A STRAMIT JACKET

FIVE HUNDRED BIRMINGHAM HOUSES INCORPORATE STRAMIT

MANY NEW SCHOOLS ARE ROOFED WITH STRAMIT

TO DISCUSS A USE FOR

STRAMIT BOARDS

CALL, WRITE OR PHONE

STOWMARKET 450

WORKS MANAGER EH GASCOINE

The wording on the above display

airfield. The Stramit side of the business was transferred from Stowmarket to Eye in 1963 and the Uxbridge side of the business (Linden Doors) was transferred to Stowmarket, although the site was really too big for joinery.

From a foreword by Torsten in a pamphlet produced in 1957, which looked back over the company's growth over the first ten years: "Throughout the ten years our factory has been at Stowmarket, and the sales office at Uxbridge. Mrs Edna **Carnell** - formerly Edna **Forsdyke** - has been at the Stowmarket office from the beginning; George **Calledyne**, Cecil **Bugg**, Louis **Maken** and Frank **Waspe** have also put in ten years' service there in varying capacities; and E. H. (Jack) **Gascoine** has been works manager since 1949. Usually to be found at the Uxbridge office are Frank **King** and Torsten J **Mosesson**, who have been directors of the company from its inception, general manager John **Souhami**, who joined in 1948, Ron **Gifford**, technical service manager (1949), Jim **Marsh** (1950), who as assistant secretary handles accounts and orders, and Harold **Joynes** (1953), who has taken on the duties of a public relations officer."

At its peak, the Stowmarket site gave work to over three hundred people with seven machines producing flat-roofing and partitioning material for the building industry with over 350,000 houses in England being built using some of the Stowmarket products despite tough competition from rival products such as gypsum boards. 1974 proved to be a very bad year for the company: it was hit by the worst building recession ever known and there was a very poor straw harvest. Worst of all, Torsten **Mosesson**, who was a prominent figure in the business world having been awarded the Order of Vasa by the King of Sweden for services to Anglo-Swedish business as well as being Chairman of the Swedish Chamber of Commerce, President of the British Door Association, President of the English Joinery Manufacturers Association, a director of the Building Centre and who sat on many other committees, died suddenly and unexpectedly aged sixty-seven.

On the death of his father, John **Mosesson** was elected chairman of the group. Having studied at Keele University and the Royal College of Music, John had come to Suffolk to teach music in 1965. He had become well-acquainted with Stowmarket over the years being sent from the family home in London during his holidays to do jobs around the Stramit site like "breaking up old railway wagons or chipping cement off used bricks as part of my correction training." It was while teaching music at Suffolk Rural Music School in Ipswich that John took an interest in an unusual blind-making machine on the Stramit site which had been used for making blinds to fit the group's Tomo windows. Since the window production had discontinued, John saw an opportunity to sell the Swedish pleated blinds to the market generally and bought the plant from the family. John then went into the business in 1966 independently from his family and with his colleague Ken **Read** from Ipswich, built up '**Sampson** Blinds.' Forty people are employed at T F **Sampson** Ltd. today. Significant events in the company's history have included becoming a supplier to Habitat, pioneering pleated blinds for conservatories and introducing remote radio-controlled and wind and sun-sensitive operations for blinds and awnings. When in 1974 John took on the family business, the two groups were for a while run as one. In 1982 it was decided to rationalise. John's three brothers Michael, Anders and Lars took on the property side of the business (Tomo Business Park) and John amalgamated T F **Sampson** Ltd. and Stramit. The three brothers now all live in Suffolk where they have brought up their families and take an active part in their respective communities.

Ernest Humphries (Jack) **Gascoine**, who had been an engineer in the Royal Air Force working mostly on Hawker Hurricanes, remembers applying to Torsten at the Uxbridge factory in 1948 when he was de-mobilised from the Services and was offered the post of engineering manager at the fledgling Stowmarket site. Jack says that when he took on the job, there were only two Swedish-made 'Motala' machines (Nos 1 & 2) of which only one was working an eight hour day. There was an important development in 1949 when Jack was appointed Engineer/Manager and immediately introduced the use of resin glue as a stronger adhesive between the paper covering and the straw, the resin being supplied by Messrs CIBA of Duxford. The engineering shop was enlarged and Bob **Cousins** was engaged as draughtsman to assist in re-developing the main machine and cut-off saw and end-seal mechanism. John **Souhami** and Ron **Gifford** at Uxbridge worked to increase the awareness of Stramit to the building industry. Whilst Jack was manager at the factory up to six machines were built enabling twenty-four hour working, producing one thousand tons per week. Between 1950 and 1955 two more Swedish-made machines (Nos 3 & 4) were installed. From 1955 to 1960 three more machines (Nos 5, 6 & 7) were added, with number 6 machine being housed in a separate part of the site for research and development. When the company started making plans to move to Eye, new British-made machines were ordered from Messrs **Halls**, Engineers of Shrewsbury. Jack left the company for a few years but in 1968 was appointed as Technical Director to the Tomo Trading Co which involved him in travelling around to many countries selling the Stramit products and helping to set up manufacturing sites. Jack was responsible for the machines sent abroad and for their installation, as well as on-site training of the personnel. The Stowmarket number 6 machine went to the Eye complex but the other Stowmarket machines were spread around the world after they were cleared from the production shop. Machines numbered 1 & 2 (the oldest) were stored for a while before being scrapped. Number 3 was sold to Mexico, number 4 went to Sri Lanka, number 5 went to Thailand and number 7 went to Spain. Later some of the machines from Eye also found their way to far-flung places so that Stramit board production could be made all round the world. Stramit had plants on every continent with boards being made in North and South America, Africa, Australia, New Zealand and even Russia, as well as several sites thoughout Europe. Stowmarket-made Stramit boards were exported to the Middle-East and the Far-East and could even be found on the Falkland Islands.

Today, Stramit International, like so many other UK manufacturing companies, has moved its production interests overseas, notably to the Czech Republic for Europe and China for Asia. However, the experience gained from fifty years' research, development and production in Suffolk, today forms the basis of Stramit International's main business, the exporting of a modern building material technology in the form of licence, trademark, plant, know-how and training. Much of that experience and know-how is to be found in the hands of a special and dedicated group of people in Stowmarket and the region who have worked for the **Mosesson's** and Stramit during the formative years. ❑

stramit INTERNATIONAL

J Nunn & Son

A Kelly's directory dated 1888 lists two bootmakers in Union Street: these were Charles **Bedser** and Brice **Tydeman**. In an 1892 directory Mr **Bedser** had moved his business to New Bond Street and in place of Mr **Tydeman** appears Jonathan **Nunn**.

Jonathan (John) **Nunn** was born in Tan Office Lane, Chevington near Bury St. Edmunds 12th May 1868, son of Josiah and Eliza **Nunn** (née **Newman**). He was educated at Chevington School, leaving at the age of thirteen. For pocket money the young John worked as a gamekeeper's boy for the Marquis of Bristol on the Ickworth Estate. The 1881 census lists the family (all of whom were born in the village) as: Josiah, aged forty-four, agricultural labourer; Eliza, his wife, age forty-one, a tailoress; daughter Eliza, aged twenty-one and also a tailoress; James, aged seventeen and Jonathan, aged thirteen, both agricultural labourers; Georgiana, aged eleven, Julia, aged eight and Martin, aged seven, all scholars, with Rose, aged four and Alice, aged ten months. Two younger daughters, Sarah and Janet, were born later. It was probably at this time that John began working alongside John **Argent**, a shoemaker in the village; indeed, the 1881 census shows the **Argent** family as shoemakers in several of the neighbouring villages. Up to this time the only choice people had were hand-made shoes or nothing, but the early 1880's saw the first pairs of factory-made shoes being made generally available.

Jonathan Nunn, circa 1890

In 1888, at the age of nineteen and after serving his apprenticeship, John moved to Stowmarket where he started work for Brice **Tydeman**. Not long after his twentieth birthday he had the opportunity to take over the business, so he made an offer that was duly accepted. The 1891 census shows John, aged twenty-two, a master shoemaker, boarding with Brice and Mary Ann **Tydeman** in Bury Street. John's first boot and shoe making premises was situated on the corner of Union Street and Brewery Row (currently a private house) and very soon he had five people working for him. One of these men was Charlie **Chester**, who was reputed to walk from Barking Tye every day, make two pairs of boots (declining to stop for meal breaks on most days) and then return home every evening. John was an early member

The Salvation Army Band outside their first meeting house in Brewery Row

of the Salvation Army, which used to meet at rooms the opposite end of Brewery Row to his workshop. His involvement with the Salvation Army did not have very honourable beginnings, as he was first a member of the Skeleton Army. This was a band of people who would jostle, heckle and generally be abusive to the fledgling group of Salvationists as they marched and sang in the town. However, John's conscience eventually won through and he joined up, quickly becoming a member of the band and soon leading them as their first commissioned Bandmaster. He then learnt what it was like to be on the receiving end of the Skeleton Army's attentions when, during one open-air meeting, his cornet was pushed into his face breaking one of his teeth. Whilst he was a member of the Salvationists he wrote several pieces of music, some of which were published by the Salvation Army and used in their song books. Jonathan **Nunn**, aged twenty-three, married Hannah **Prentice**, aged twenty, at Stowmarket Register Office on 24th October 1891. They had five children whilst at their first house in Union Street: Lily, born 8th June 1893; Maud, born 28th June 1894; Jonathan (Jack), born 18th April 1895; Rose Mary, born 5th May 1899 and Frank, born 25th December 1901. In 1907 the family moved to 55, Union Street, premises that had previously been the Candle Factory, also known as 'Tallow Hall', founded by Robert **Bond** and later owned by William George **Balls**. At about this time John left the Salvation Army and joined the Methodist Church in Regent Street. Wray Josiah **Nunn** was born at 55, Union Street on 24th October 1910. The business continued to be built up and Jack and Rose both helped their father by repairing hand-made shoes, especially during the period of the First World War. Because John was left-handed, the knives and tools with which he used to cut and work

Nunn's first premises in Union Street. Charlie Chester is 2nd from left & John, with moustache, is standing in the doorway

the leather became worn in such a manner, that consequently other members of the family could not use the majority of these tools. It was a highly skilled business with in-house training. The best leather was used for dress-shoes, the whole shoe being hand stitched. No surgical alterations were done there to boots and shoes, although extra side-linings were occasionally added where needed. Customers regularly came from as far afield as Finningham, Old Newton and Debenham, but even when people moved further away from the area, for example to Canada and Australia, they would still ask for their shoes to be made by **Nunn's**. This was known as 'continuing trade'. John used to point out to people that everybody had odd feet, but would add, "it was better than being odd at the other end".

Wray attended local schools and upon leaving in 1924 at the age of fourteen, alongside his father, he began to learn the

The Nunn family in their garden in Union Street circa 1911 (standing l. to r.) Jonathan jnr (Jack) & Rose Mary (seated l. to r.) Jonathan snr (John), Maud & Hannah (née Prentice) holding Wray and Frank with dog

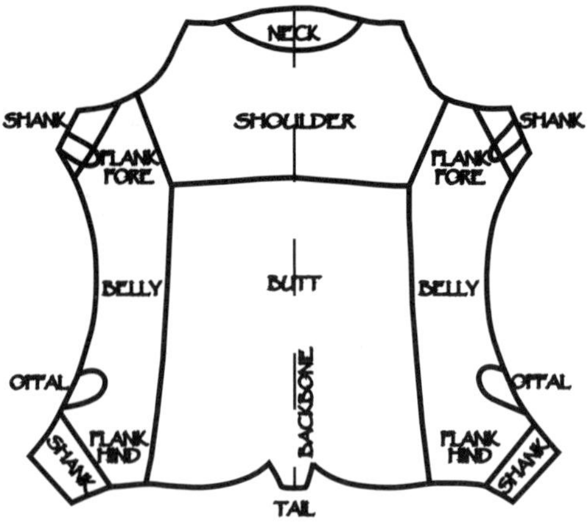

The division of a butt of leather

skills needed for making boots and shoes. The leather was bought from Tanneries, including Combs. When the neck and legs were removed, this was called a "butt" (half a lengthways "butt" was known as a "bend"). Leather was tanned and dressed (stuffed with grease) according to the purpose for which it was used. If the tannage was right, leather was available for every specific part of the shoe: the best inner soles came from the belly leather, as it sustained a crosswise pull; side-liners were cut from upper leather. The rump leather was harder wearing and more suitable for abrasive wear. It should be remembered that leather varies in the same degree as cuts of meat. Sole leather, being measured in "irons", was bought by the weight and upper leather was bought by area and substance. Soles were cut from the bends according to the wearer's requirement, endeavouring to match, where the most wear was likely to be, to the hardest wearing part of the leather. More than one pair of boots or shoes was worked at a time, providing a sequence of preparation, development and fitting. The leather for the uppers was cut from skins of calf and kid, into the various shapes (toecap, quarters, lace hole panels and tongue etc.) that were then stitched together. The inner soles would be thoroughly wetted and stretched over a last (a wooden form in the shape of a foot) and allowed to completely dry out. It was then trimmed to thc shapc of the last and the edges were feathered to take the welt. The welts, which were cut from 'greasy welt shoulders' were sewn on, using horizontal seams and allowed to dry until quite rigid. The upper was then placed on a last and moulded to the required shape by being drawn tightly over the last and tacked into place. "Lasting tacks" were hand-made nails bought from the Birmingham area. The next part of the process was 'bottoming' (stitching the selected sole to the uppers), then the heel was added before the 'finishing' (cleaning and polishing)

John Nunn with his prize gourds

In the garden of 55 Union Street. (standing) John with Frank, (sitting) Rose and Wray

John at work in his Union Street premises

John Nunn at work

completed the procedure. One pair of boots could normally be produced in a day. It was usual for shoemakers to make their own flax and hemp threads (up twenty-six cord) for hand stitching, flax being used for shoes and hemp for heavyweight work, like boots. Shoemaker's wax was made from a mixture of pitch, tallow, resin and beeswax and was very sticky. The ingredients would be altered at different times of the year to suit the weather conditions, more tallow in winter to help soften it and more resin in summer to stop it being too soft. The workshop had to be kept warm to keep the waxed threads pliable as well as the friction from drawing through the hands to keep them supple. Holes were made by an awl and the ends of the threads were tapered with a hog's bristle attached as a rigid guide to ease the thread though. As the temperature in the workshop often did not reach the required level during the daytime, most of this hand sewing was done in the evening, by the light of an oil lamp which was suspended from the ceiling. Wray recalls being told by his father how, when customers commented how easy it looked to draw threads though the awled holes, he would offer them the chance to try for themselves. He would, however, get the warmed thread part way through a hole, then allow it to cool sufficiently for the wax to solidify and tighten itself in the hole, making it virtually impossible to pull through until it was warmed again (which the unsuspecting person would not know).

The trade stamp **'J NUNN'** was imprinted in the waist of every boot and shoe and the largest pair that Wray can remember ever having been made on the premises was size thirteen. Lap shoes or lap boots, which have the tongue stitched beneath the lace holes, ensuring a waterproof seal, were made from the whole hide for farm worker's use. Between the wars, a pair of boots would be made for two weeks' of a farm labourer's wages. At that time a labourer received thirty shillings (£1:50) a week, so a pair of boots would cost him three pounds.

John Nunn in the sidecar being driven by his niece's husband Arthur Rolfe of Chevington

Wray Nunn playing his Parkington bass

Wray, like his father, was also very interested in music and started on piano lessons, but quickly decided that that instrument was not for him. He was sent to buy a double bass and he said 'it was love at first sight'. His first instrument, a three-stringed bass, was bought for £4 in 1927 from **Cole's** furniture shop in the town. His next bass was bought for £10, although worth over £60, and was made in 1902 by Jeffery J. **Gilbert** of Peterborough, originally for John P. **Parkington** and was the only bass that Mr **Gilbert** made, as it had been part of a set of musical instruments made for the **Parkington** family. Wray started to play alongside other members of his family with the small string orchestra at the local Methodist Chapel.

John passed the business over to Wray just prior to the outbreak of the Second World War. On the 9th September 1939, six days after war was declared, Wray married Beryl Evelyn **Pratt** of Melton near Woodbridge.

Jonathan and Hannah Nunn (née Prentice)

Wray's mother, Hannah, died 17th February 1940 just prior to her first grandson, Jonathon, being born later that year. Wray was called up on 11th December 1941; his father tried to carry on with the business, but found it was too much to manage single-handed. Another contributory factor to this was the reduction in the allocation of leather by the Board of Trade and the business was therefore closed for the duration of the war. Wray and Beryl's second son, David, was born in 1942. During this period, Wray was called to Ilfracombe in Devon and invited to join and tour with the 'Western Command Symphony Orchestra'.

A pair of Wray Nunn's own hand-made shoes with the lasts on which they were formed as well as a few tools of the trade

A view of 55 Union Street (formerly known as Cats Lane)

A close-up of the board above the window at 55 Union Street, where the wording J Nunn & Son can still just be seen

Wray's father, Jonathan **Nunn** senior, died in an ambulance on the way to hospital on 5th December 1944 aged seventy-six. Wray was 'demobbed' in 1945 and tried to re-establish the business. Their third son, Stephen, was born in 1946. The business in Union Street (this part is also known as Cats Lane) continued for several more years into the early 1950's; many people may remember the unusual and informative window displays showing the various stages of boot and shoe construction. Due to the dramatic increase in mass-produced, factory-made shoes, the demand for quality hand-made footwear declined, so the business closed in 1956.

Wray and his family moved to Hertford where he took up a position teaching his trade at the William **Baker** Technical School. As a result of his freelancing, his musical prowess became known and he joined the Royal Ballet orchestra as a regular extra. In 1968 when the William **Baker** Technical School closed, he was called by Covent Garden to play full-time for the Royal Ballet. In this capacity, he had the honour to play for such professional dancers as Margot **Fonteyn** and Rudolph **Nureyev**. Wray and his family moved back to Suffolk in 1987, buying a bungalow in the village of Barrow near Bury St Edmunds. Wray finally stopped playing professionally in 1998.

Today, leather is no longer the main material used in shoemaking: canvas, cotton and many synthetic substances are also used. Many shoe-manufacturing operations are automated and shoes may be designed on a computer, components being cut by a laser and stitched by computer-controlled stitchers. Such improvements enable manufacturers to respond to style changes quickly, in order to follow fleeting fashion trends, which is far removed from when it was a necessity to have a pair of boots or shoes that you knew would last for several years. ❑

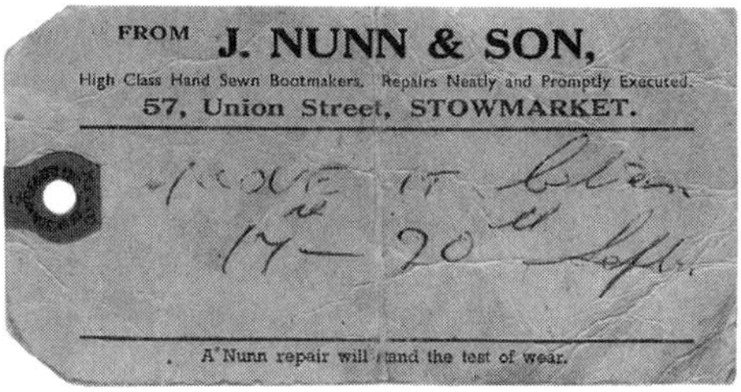

W H Pike & Sons

When William Herbert **Pike** moved with his family from King's Road, Chelsea to Stowmarket in 1927, the plot of land next to George E. **Cobbold's** (of Battisford) blacksmith's forge in Combs Ford was a piece of waste ground which adjoined the Gladstone Arms public house. At that time the forge was managed by Mr W. **Tolworthy** and from 1938 by Frank William **Stammers**, as working blacksmiths. However, it was here that William **Pike** decided to start his business and the garage, pumps and workshops that were built here began trading in 1928. William had been born April 22nd 1883 into a family that had run a successful charabanc and transport business in the Chelsea area since 1840. The business, founded by William Joseph **Pike** and trading as W. J. **Pike** Ltd, dealt with all aspects of the business including a farrier's shop. By the 1920's William H. had chosen to move to the cleaner air of the country with his wife Philomena, born 1885, and sons William J (Bill) born 1909 and Andrew, born 1912. There were also three daughters namely: Violet born 1907, Mena and Doris. In the 1933 Kelly's directory their entry is listed as '**Pike**, W. H. & Son, motor engineers, Combs Ford. TN Stowmarket 96.'

The early business originally consisted of sales and repairs to motorcycles, expanding later to include cars, as well as petrol, oil, tyres and other vehicular services. Later the business diversified again to include a small fleet of haulage lorries which consisted of one ten-tonner and one tipper, together with about six other smaller trucks. During the war period the haulage work was extended. The majority of their work was providing services to supply road chippings, shingle and sand from local gravel pits for the Suffolk County Council for the making up and repairing of the B-class roads in the area. Sugar beet was hauled from local farms to the two sugar processing factories nearby thoughout the autumn and winter months. Frank **Stammers**' son, John, born 1926, began working for **Pike's** in 1941 and started in the garage, when, after a few months, he was asked to help as a mate to Cyril **Mannall** on the lorries. This quickly became his full-time post for two and a half years until he enlisted in the army in 1944. He remembers the lorries being used to take coal and coke from Stowmarket railway station to Wattisham Airfield. He says that the lorries were all Leyland models and named after

An early view of the garage showing the original façade

Bill Pike outside the garage in the 1930's

animals, such as Beaver, Badger and Retriever etc. John also remembers that during the wartime blackouts, the sugar beet lorries often had to have a man sitting on each wing to help the driver navigate along the unlit country roads. John also states that his father was often given the job of repairing vehicle springs from the garage.

Philomena died in 1953, aged sixty-nine, at their bungalow called 'Mandalay' in Combs Lane. The following year, thirty-six year old Ella **Boast** started to work for the business after leaving the employment of the Co-op where she had been working in various departments, including the butchery cash desk, for fifteen years. Her duties were clerical and payroll etc. Ella says that her father, Sid **Boast**, had briefly worked for the fledgling garage within the first year of its opening, but he decided that the

Stowmarket Motor-Cycle Club outside the garage in 1929. Some of the people and motor-cycles pictured have been identified as follows: (from r.) Matchless - Charlie Scarf, AJS, AJS 2¾ h.p. - W J Pike, AJS - Mr Chappel, ???, BSA - Percy Kensal, BSA, AJS 3½ h.p. - Joe Stearn.

TELEPHONE—
96 STOWMARKET

APPOINTED GARAGE

Cars driven by our staff at owner's risk only

MEMO.
from
W. H. PIKE & SONS,
A.M. INST., B.E.
Motor Engineers,
Bridge Garage, COMBS FORD,
STOWMARKET.

Cars • Commercial Vehicles • Motor Cycles

CARS AND LORRIES SUPPLIED — CASH OR HIRE PURCHASE
—
HAULAGE CONTRACTORS
—
REPAIRS AND OVERHAULS
—
UNDER PERSONAL SUPERVISION

A Pike's letterhead from the 1930's

work was not to his liking and moved on. However, Ella's loyalty was more lasting, as she stayed with the business for twenty-five years. Ella remembers that although William was already past normal retirement age, he continued to keep his hands on the reins as much as possible for as long as he could, but finally relinquished the running of the business to his sons, Andrew and Bill, in 1958. One of their first decisions was to extend the showroom to sell new and second-hand cars. It was during this period that they employed over thirty people which included petrol pump attendants, workshop mechanics, haulage vehicle drivers, as well as Ella in the office. Bill is remembered as being the engineer and often was seen in his grubby brown smock whilst Andrew was the car salesman and wore a suit to work. **Pike's** carried out M.O.T vehicle testing, they were Automobile Association (AA) and Royal Automobile Club (RAC) registered as well as serving the town with breakdown cover with their Land Rover towing vehicle. There being no other garages of this size in the vacinity allowed **Pike's** to serve the whole town and surrounding area. However, due to changing trends, the haulage business was sold in 1967. It should also be remembered that a driving school service was provided from the premises and several people may have learned their driving skills with Ollie **Lodge**, one of the driving instructors who started at **Pike's** before setting up his own school of motoring. William H. **Pike** died January 1968 aged eighty-three.

In 1978, four years after the death of Andrew **Pike** at the age of sixty-two, the business was sold to J. G. **Wright** and became known as **Pike's**, Bridge Garage. Most of the staff was retained, including Ella, but she decided to have a change of career, so after overseeing the transitional period, she started work at Woolpit Health Centre. George **Hunting** was the manager of the garage at this time.

A twin-axled lorry built by Pike's for R Baker and Son, millers, of Elmswell

John **Wright** had been trained at O. G **Barnard** and Sons from 1944. In 1956, however, he decided to go into business on his own and set up a garage at Great Finborough with the franchise for Austin and Ford vehicles. He branched out briefly to a garage at Saxmundham for four years but then, in 1964, he purchased **Scarff's** garage in Bury Street, Stowmarket. He demolished the old premises in 1968 and built new workshops and showrooms on the site in 1973. A year after acquiring Pike's garage, he merged all his businesses with **Thurlow's** Ltd., maintaining a fifty per cent interest and the garage became the **Thurlow Pike** Garage and had the Vauxhall-Opel dealership. By 1986 all of John **Wright's** garages were bought by the **Thurlow Nunn Standen** Group. However, the Combs Ford site was then bought by the Esso company, whose petrol had been sold at the garage from the very early days of the business and in that year the old showrooms and workshops were demolished as the new self-service pump forecourt and shop facility were built. Other members of staff

Uncle Frank with Pike's first coach

Pike's garage in the 1950's.
Note the Suffolk Iron Foundry articulated lorry in the background

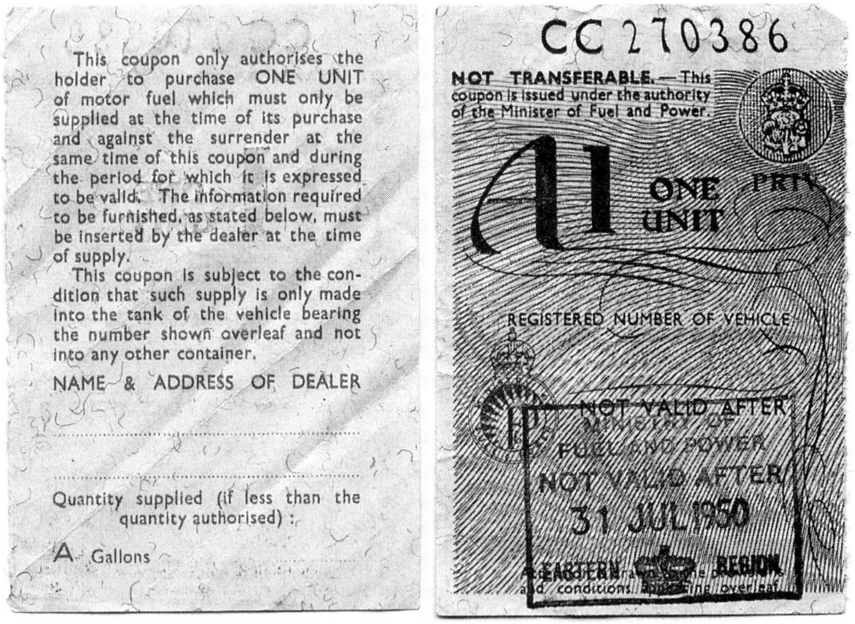
This coupon only authorises the holder to purchase ONE UNIT of motor fuel which must only be supplied at the time of its purchase and against the surrender at the same time of this coupon and during the period for which it is expressed to be valid. The information required to be furnished, as stated below, must be inserted by the dealer at the time of supply.

This coupon is subject to the condition that such supply is only made into the tank of the vehicle bearing the number shown overleaf and not into any other container.

NAME & ADDRESS OF DEALER

....

....

Quantity supplied (if less than the quantity authorised) :

A Gallons

CC 270386

NOT TRANSFERABLE.—This coupon is issued under the authority of the Minister of Fuel and Power.

A1 ONE UNIT

REGISTERED NUMBER OF VEHICLE

NOT VALID AFTER

MINISTRY OF FUEL AND POWER

NOT VALID AFTER

31 JUL 1950

EASTERN REGION

A Ministry of Fuel & Power fuel coupon from 1950 used to obtain fuel from Pike's garage whilst rationing was still in force following WWII

included Ken **Ash**, Charlie **Broom**, Cedric **Brackenbury**, Ray **Bullett**, Ian **Button**, Alan **Carter**, Raymond **Francis**, Neddy **Hales**, Chris **Last**, Jack **Mayhew**, Stan **Mayhew**, Harry **Meakins**, Paul **Oakley**, Harry **Rush**, Len **Savill**, George **Shave**, Harold **Turner**, John **Turner**, Les **Waters**, Ivan **Woods** and Reg **Youngs**.

Harry **Rush** had been bom in 1927 and started work at **Pike's** in 1941 aged fourteen, staying for three and a half years until 1945 when he joined the Army. Upon his return in 1948, he then worked for O G **Barnard** and Sons for seven years, then after a brief move to Norfolk, returned to Old Newton and began working at **Pike's** once more, where he stayed for a further twenty seven years. Harry worked in the paint shop, which was a prefabricated building next to the wall of the Gladstone Arms, alongside Len **Savill** and Harry **Vert**. Harry (**Rush**) and Len were the spray painters and Harry (**Vert**) was the brush painter. This team painted the liveries on the bodyworks made by carpenters in the garage's workshops for Eastern Electricity, Stowmarket Meat Traders and the Suffolk Iron Foundry lorries etc. Harry remembers, when he was a petrol boy, witnessing the American petrol tanker taking the corner too fast and crashing into a C.W.S milk tanker and killing its driver, Albert **Goodchild**, in May 1944. The contents of the petrol tanker caught fire and the flaming liquid ran back towards the garage, but fortunately dispersed into a culvert and ditch leading to the river before reaching the garage's own petrol tanks, which were the only source of petrol in the town during the war. Harry also remembers Bill **Pike's** passion for greyhounds, including training and racing etc. and says that he occasionally was asked to help with their exercise. This involved a modified bicycle that had metal spikes where the seat and handlebars should be so, that it could be inverted and stuck in the ground of the meadow opposite. A long line was attached to the tyre-less rim of the rear wheel and extended across the meadow and had a rabbit skin tied to the end. Harry's job was then to hand-crank the pedals round, causing the skin to be dragged across the grass with the greyhounds in pursuit. This field was also used for a week every summer to host a travelling fair. Bill's contribution to this event was to renovate and overhaul the generator which provided power for the lights and rides etc. A later development, Harry mentions, is the panel repair work and spraying on Lambretta scooters that **Pike's** did for **Revett's** motor cycle and scooter business in Ipswich Street from the mid 1950's.

A twin-axled lorry supplied by Pike's to the Stowmarket Timber Co.

Jack **Mayhew** came out of the Services in 1947, applied for a job at the garage and as it was Bill **Pike's** policy to employ ex-servicemen, he readily obtained work as a lorry driver, staying for twenty-five years. Jack remembers that his main job was loading and delivering coal and coke which was collected from the Railway Station, shovelled by hand and delivered to Wattisham Airfield, where it was then unloaded, again by hand. On many occasions after loading, the lorry, when negotiating the turning from Station Road into the Market Place, would sometimes spill some of its load causing several people to scramble for a few odd nuggets of coal to supplement their wartime rations. Jack later did contract work on alternate days of the week, which took him all over East Anglia for a London company with a depot at the Old Maltings in Prentice Road. Still using the **Pike's** lorry, his loads were mostly tiled fireplaces, bathroom suites, floor tiles and guttering etc. These lorries boasted the new self-starters and side windows, but were still cold enough to warrant the wearing of the old army greatcoat for warmth during the winter months. Jack also worked for a time in the greasing bay, before leaving in 1972.

Another example of a Pike's twin-axled lorry

Stan **Mayhew** (no relation to Jack) started work at the garage just after the war when he was demobbed from the RAF. His first job was as a driver and he remembers the

A Leyland six-wheeled tipper on sale at Pike's

lorries were ex-army Leyland and Austin six-wheeler trucks and as well as the previously mentioned loads, they also used to collect chalk from the Needham Market chalk pits and deliver it around the county to be spread on the land. He later went into the garage and worked alongside the carpenters by making the ironwork bracing for the bodywork on lorry bucks etc. Stan says that the lorries had the **Pike's** name on boards mounted on the cabs and later had sign-written names on the door panels.

Ray **Bullett** joined the company in 1951 and worked there for fourteen years. He started a five-year apprenticeship as a mechanic, learning the trade from people such as Jack **Wade**. Ray recalls the frequent floods that occured in Combs Ford which often affected parts of the garage workshops and also having to tow stranded vehicles out of quite deep water near **Boulter's** Bridge on numerous occasions. He also remembers having to recover damaged vehicles from accidents, especially from black-spots such as Badley Hill.

A Jaguar car leaving the forecourt

Len **Savill** (Deafy) started work at the garage as a long driver's mate in 1942 but soon got work in the garage, thanks to Andrew **Pike**. Len was an accomplished paint sprayer and also did panelwork, making up body work for local firms' lorry fleets. During a slack period at the garage in the early 1940's, Len briefly went to work for **Moy's** coal merchants and was on the lorry alongside his brother Alf, but eventually returned to the garage where he stayed for forty-four years. His brother, Alf, joined him at the garage for about a year before

Another view of the garage probably dating from the late 1960's

moving on. Len also remembers the American tanker lorry crashing and the burning petrol reaching the forecourt, necessitating many vehicles to be moved and some being damaged. He also mentioned the regular flooding and added that the water would come in one end of the building and flow out of the other. Tools and other items had to be quickly gathered up and put at a higher level and then they would have to go home, as the workshops would be unusable. Len says that he worked with Ivan **Bolton**, Percy **Wade** and Harold **Turner** and that they were a happy gang in a very friendly, family-like environment. Len says that the whole garage turned out to watch the Queen go past when she visited the town in 1961, commenting on how young she looked. He mentioned that Bill **Pike**, who smoked a pipe, had a narrow escape when part of a crane jib broke off and fell, snapping the end off his pipe while it was in his mouth as he stood near a pit used to work on the undersides of cars.

Roger **Miles** started working for **Pike's** as a fifteen year-old school-leaver in 1955, biking from his home in Wyverstone. He worked in the garage on car maintenance and repairs and his duties also included pump work on the forecourt, which involved taking cash payments for the petrol through to the office. In May 1960, however, he was called up to do his National Service, but would visit his old workmates when home on leave. On his discharge in November 1962, he returned to the garage, but asked if he could be taken on as a lorry driver. Along with the other drivers the bulk of his work was mainly carting coal or sugar beet. He also had to collect bags of cement from Claydon Cement Works and remembers that on hot days the bags came directly off the production line and were almost too hot to handle. Extras duties would be asked of him when he had to go further afield to places such as King's Lynn or Wells, where he would be expected to release some of Bill **Pike's** homing pigeons, with strict instructions to "bring the box back". He also had to run errands for Andrew to buy his '3 Castles' brand of cigarettes from **Durrant's** the Newsagency and sausages from the London Meat Company, both of which were in Ipswich Street. Roger states that the larger vehicle parts were stored in a building close to the Boys' Brigade building in Combs Lane which meant occasionally having to trundle heavy items across the road. Another abiding memory that has stayed with Roger is when he was asked to take a bus ride to **Botwood's** Garage in Ipswich to pick up a rear spring for a lorry. The spring was so well greased that when he tried to board a bus for the return journey he was refused access. He then had to go to a stationers near to the bus-depot and buy a large sheet of brown paper to wrap it in. When the haulage business was sold in 1967, Roger went back to servicing cars for a while, but then decided to move the Rountson Group, a locally based firm of builders' merchants in Prentice Road, which later moved its site to Rougham, where Roger became foreman and ultimately, manager.

In 1953 Ian **Button** moved from Saxmundham, where he had begun his career in motor-mechanics at **Mitchell's** garage, to Stowmarket at the age of twenty-one. He began working for **Pike's**, lodging at the Cedars Farm for three years. Ian remembered there were over thirty people working at the garage when he joined the 'family-like team' as a mechanic, working under John **Taylor** and the working day was from 7:00am to 6:00pm from Monday to Saturday. Ian emphasised the cosy atmosphere in the garage when he mentioned the 'Suffolk' Air-Flow coke-stove where he and many of his colleagues would cook toasted cheese sandwiches on toasting forks, as well as some of the pranks played on each other, such as a five-inch steel ball being anonymously rolled towards unsuspecting victims. Due to the fact that the lorries used for the haulage side of the business had been purchased as second-hand, they were occasionally prone to breaking down, meaning that Ian would have to travel sometimes long distances to repair them. Two particular instances that came to memory were changing a differential at Wolverhampton and a gearbox outside Brixton Prison. From 1972, Ian along with Harold **Turner**, began organising works dinner-dances attended by Bill and Andrew and members of the **Pike** family and many of the staff and their wives etc. These events were held at St Peter's Church Hall in Milton Road and included live music supplied by various

Bill and Andrew Pike with a Jaguar car in the 1970's

Pike's garage prior to being bought by J G Wright

bands. These annual dances proved to be very successful and Ian and Harold continued running them until 1982, despite the fact that they had both left the garage in 1979. This was when they started up their own business as **Button** and **Turner** in a workshop leased from the Co-op behind the petrol-filling station, near **Page's** fish shop in Combs Lane. Harold retired through ill health in 1983; Ian carried on by himself until 1987 when another ex-**Pike's** man, Raymond **Francis**, became a partner. In January 1988, Ian and Raymond moved their vehicle maintenance and repair business to Gladstone Car Centre next to **Cracknell's** fish and chip shop, Needham Road when the Co-op site was cleared for the Solar supermarket development. Ian **Button** retired in 1997; Raymond took over the business and is still trading today.

Raymond **Francis** mentions a couple of the humorous memories of his time at **Pike's**, which include birthday bumps on a wet sponge and the occasion when Chris **Last**, who normally had a severe stammer, managed to reproach Ian **Button** without faltering, as he had climbed into one of Chris's freshly valetted cars while under the influence of a few drinks after spending Christmas Eve lunchtime in a nearby pub.

William J. **Pike** died in December 1994 aged eighty-five, marking the end of an era for both the family and the business. However, their legacy to the town remains, as that small corner of Combs Ford will for ever be **Pike's** corner and although it was never owned by the family, the meadow opposite is now also known as **Pike's** Meadow. ❑

Ivan Woods serving on the last day petrol was sold at the garage

GENERAL STORE

Proctor's

Sidney Charles **Proctor** was born in London in 1911, the son of Samuel **Proctor** and Alice Jane **Featherstone**. By 1915 the family had moved to Poplar Hill, Combs, where Samuel c1904, Winifred, c1908, Sidney 1911, Robert, 1915, Frederick William, 1917, Eva, 1918, Doreen, 1921, Grace, 1925 and Olive 1929 were all born. In 1934, Sidney became manager for Charles H. B. **Jaques**, confectioner, at his small shop selling sweets and tobacco at 6-8 Station Road (currently Tower Music and the William **Goodwin** Properties Estate agency). On 20th April the following year he married Olivia Sarah **Barrett**, daughter of Samuel **Barrett**, at Stowmarket Church. After a short while Sidney and Olivia moved into a second shop, which was in Stowupland Street adjacent to **Codd's** bicycle shop. This shop, which was later to become **Hopgood's** paint and wallpaper department, sold the same products, as well as ice-cream etc. His third move was to 2 Regent Street where he appears in the 1955 directory of the town and also at 51 Stowupland Street, both of which are considered to be part of the same property. In 1958, he bought these premises which had formerly been Rufus **Terry's** the harness maker; here he and Olivia traded sweets, tobacco and general provisions until December 1972. Many people will remember that Olivia made ice cream to her own recipe. Containers of ice used to come by rail twice a week in a tin-lined box; other ingredients included dried egg, butter and custard powder. She also made lemonade from fresh lemons and citric acid, selling it by the tumbler full so that customers were able to drink it in the shop. On really hot days, a scoop of ice-cream was added to the drink. She also made toffee from soft brown sugar and butter in the Swiss-roll tins, which was then broken up and sold loose. Toffee-apples were either sold plain or dipped in coconut.

The Stowupland Street premises when it was occupied by Rufus Terry's saddlers and harness makers business (photo circa 1914)

Sidney had many other fields of interest which kept him fully occupied. His love of Stowmarket and its people was expressed by being actively involved in the community. He helped to erect the grandstand at the Cricket Meadow football field, where he was also a groundsman and linesman. A weak heart prevented him from going to war, but he served as an A.R.P. (Air-Raid Patrol) warden and first-aider. He worked on the land at **Steel's** Farm (now Ashes Farm) Newton Road and also ran a private hire taxi service. As a part of the National War effort, Sidney was also involved in ploughing up the Stowmarket Golf Course so that it could be planted with crops. From about 1939, for about twenty years, Sidney leased Northfield Wood at Onehouse from Mr **Stubbs**. During this time he managed the wood by means of selective felling and coppicing; the sawn logs were then sold to local customers. He also kept free-range chickens in there, the eggs being sold in the shop. It is interesting to note that during the war, tanks, armoured cars and other military vehicles were stored there until D-Day in 1944. Sidney had the option to buy the wood for one-hundred and fifty pounds but declined the offer. The Forestry Commission then bought it in about 1960, retaining Sidney in their employment as the wood manager. His duties then included opening the wood floor by clearing brambles and light scrub, thus giving way to renewed flowering of primroses, bluebells, orchids and wild strawberries. Sidney's son, John, also joined him in this work and has given talks on the subject to various local groups.

Sidney and Olivia had four children: John (born 1936), Olive (born 1938), Roy (born 1946) and Charles (born 1950). Olive remembers first helping out in the shop from the age of eight. Her duties were cutting white paper into rectangular shapes to make into sweet bags, weighing out sugar, which was stored in large well-sealed tins, into blue paper bags both in one pound and two pound sizes, weighing half ounces and ounces of tobacco (Counter Shag, St. Julian, St. Bruno and many others), which were wrapped in pieces of paper, rolled into a tube with both ends tucked in to seal in the flavour.

Sidney Proctor helping to erect the grandstand on the former Cricket Meadow, now the site of Asda in Wilkes Way

Proctor's Stowupland Street corner shop photographed in the 1950's

The Proctor family circa 1959
(l. to r.) John, Charles, Sidney, Roy, Olive, Olivia and Peter

Robert and Sidney Proctor

Her other jobs included counting sweet coupons: category D's were two ounces (2ozs) and category E's were four ounces (4ozs) (quarter of pound) values. Nothing came pre-packed, so biscuits were weighed into half pound bags; broken biscuits were bagged up and sold cheaper. At the end of the War, Woodbine cigarettes were sold at 2½d (1p) for five, they were also sold singly at ½d each. As she got older, Olive began to serve in the shop during the school holidays and after school, but remembers having to stand on an upturned biscuit tin to reach over the counter. During this period her wage was two-shillings and six pence per week (2/6) or (12½p). When Olive left school she went into the shop full time with her parents and earned £1:10s (£1:50p) per week plus a clothing allowance.

Olive **Proctor** married Peter Henry **Edwards**, born 1934, son of Walter **Edwards** and Gertrude **Gladwell** of Nedging Tye, at Stowmarket Parish Church 9th March 1957. Olive and Peter lived at 2 Regent Street which adjoined the shop . It was at this address, in 1958, that Adrian, the first of their five children, was born: Ann 1961, Allison 1965, Adele 1970 and Amanda in 1973 all being born in Ipswich Hospital. Peter and Olive moved out of the Regent Street shop and moved to 28 Stowupland Street then moved to Cherry Tree Road for a while until they were able to buy their first house at 48 Cardinals Road.

In 1972 Sidney and Olivia moved from Regent Street into a house in Cardinals Road and Olive and Peter moved back to 2 Regent Street and took over the full running of the shop. By 1973 they had carried out a few alterations to the shop by putting in larger windows etc. and diversified their stock by selling groceries and greengrocery as well. In 1980 Sidney Charles **Proctor** died aged sixty-nine.

Olive and Peter continued to trade here until 1984, selling the business to Paula and Don **Barnard** who carried out some more refurbishments and re-named it 'The Cabin'. Olive and Peter moved on and took over the fish and chip shop on Stowupland Green, where they traded from 1987 until 1994. However, in 1990 they opened a farm shop in Combs Lane, growing and selling organic produce, a service they continued to provide until 1996, when, due to changing market trends, they decided to return to selling fish and chips, this time at The Fisherman's Basket in Wolsey Road. Olive and Peter finally retired from trading in July 2000 and moved to a bungalow at Harleston Green. Despite all their children having helped them in many ways in their varied businesses, none of them have decided to follow in their footsteps. ❑

(above) The Stowupland Street shop in 1989. (left) The view from the Stowupland Street shop as it appeared in the 'Outlook in Store' competition in the 1989 Stowmarket Carnival magazine

The fish and chip shop at Thorney Green Stowupland as it appeared in the 'Plaice the Face' competition in the 1991 Stowmarket Carnival magazine

Peter Edwards at the Stowupland fish and chip shop in 1991

G F Ray & Son

FAMILY GROCER

The first appearance of **Ray's** grocery shop in Bury Street, Stowmarket, is in the 1891 census where he is listed as George Frederick **Ray**, a master grocer aged thirty-one, born London. His wife was Kate E., aged thirty, born Stratford St Mary, with children Arthur Stanley (Stanley) aged three and Leonard George, aged one, both born in Ipswich; their third son, Owen Frederick, was born at the Bury Street premises in Stowmarket in December 1893. Unfortunately, Owen, who was married, died as a result of being gassed in 1915 during the First World War. However, in the 1881 census George is unmarried and aged twenty-one and found living at Lower Street, Stratford St Mary with his widowed mother Sarah, aged forty-eight who was born at Dedham, Essex. Both were grocer's assistants. George's future wife appears as Kate Ellen **Barber** who was aged twenty and living with her parents, William, aged fifty-two, a master carpenter and Maria his wife aged forty-five in Upper Street, Stratford St Mary. Also in the household were her brothers Albert aged ten, Sidney aged eight and Harry aged four, as well as sister Letitia, aged six. By setting up shop in 1891 it was too late for George to appear in the 1892 Kelly's directory, but he does appear by 1900 as **Ray**, George Frederick, grocer Bury Street and by 1915 the entry is the same except that the number of the premises is fifteen. The rate book for the same year shows that they were living at 17 Bury Street. The 1922 directory lists **Ray**, George Frederick & Son at the same address and in 1925 the telephone number is Stowmarket 6. The 1937 Kelly's lists the business as G. F. **Ray** & Son, grocers and provision merchants, 15 to 19 Bury Street, TN 6. These listings continued in a similar form for another thirty years through to 1967/68 but by 1969 the entry had disappeared from the town directories.

During the 1920's George, who then lived at Woodfield House, had samples of various brands of tea sent to the house for him to test and blend, as he did all of his own blending in those days. Each of about ten different types of tea were laid out in a semicircle in front of him, each one forming a small pile of tea-leaves on a sheet of paper. He would lift one of these samples and bury his nose in it, inhaling the scent for a few moments, then lay it down again on the table, pick up another pile and do the same. Then he

George Frederick Ray circa 1920

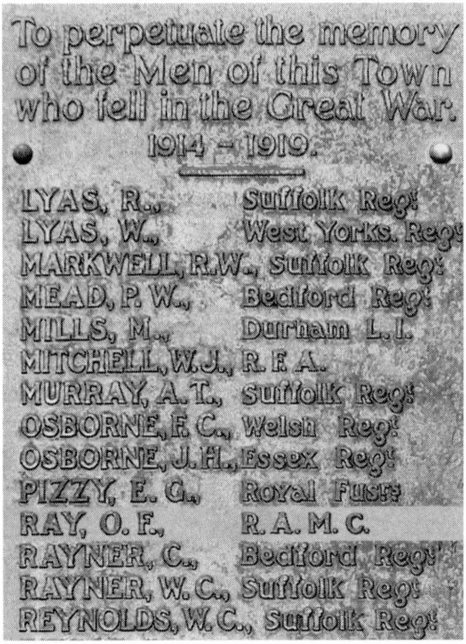

Owen Frederick Ray's name on the War Memorial Gates, Finborough Road Stowmarket

George Frederick's wife Kate E Ray (née Barber)

would take a pinch of one pile and blend it with another, making notes on a pad beside him. This would go on for an hour or more until he had decided upon exactly what blends were to be packaged and his written notes would be taken back to the shop to be made up into packets for sale. Today, at supermarkets, various brands and blends of tea can be bought depending on tastes, but the individuality of the teas blended in the shop are sadly no more. G. F. **Ray** & Son were known not only as grocers and provision merchants, but also as tea and coffee blenders.

Stanley married Evelyn Mary **Keay**, who had been born at Dulwich in 1898, (affectionately known as 'Toni') at Stowmarket Congregational Church in 1916 at 8:00am. They had three daughters Evelyn Beryl (Beryl) born October 1917, Mary Eileen (Eileen) born December 1918 and Winifred Lettie (Bunty) born November 1925. Leonard married Elsie **Ray** (no known relation) and had John Leonard (Jack) and Alan Major. Stanley was educated at Needham Market and after leaving school served his grocery apprenticeship in Dovercourt, Essex. In the 1920's Stanley became a Fellow of the Grocers' Institute and was involved with judging at the Royal Horticultural Hall in London each year, staying in Hendon with relations. Stanley once told his nephew, Jack **Ray**, son of Leonard, that he had to judge at the annual Grocers' Exhibition in London. This consisted of a side of bacon being given to each candidate for membership, and he or she had to price the various cuts so as to make a given margin of profit overall and individually. Jack, who was born 1916, also has other recollections of chatting to his uncle 'Stan'. One of these is that in his younger days **Ray's** sold three principal types of ham:- Calne (Wiltshire)

George Frederick Ray relaxing in the garden with his grandmother and Aunt Lettie circa 1930

Arthur Stanley (Stanley) and his wife Evelyn Mary (Toni) Ray (née Keay) circa 1920's

The Bury Street shop circa 1920 with the Model T Ford delivery van outside

ham, York ham and Suffolk ham. He boasted that Elmswell bacon and Suffolk ham was superior to all the others. Jack believes it was cured in black treacle, but tended to 'go off' rather more quickly than the other two types. Jack, who occasionally stayed at his uncle's shop, remembers being told of a lady who came into the shop and asked in her broad Suffolk accent for some soop and when Stanley replied "Yes, madam, would you like tomato, mulligatawny or oxtail?" "'Course not," she snapped. "Oi wants some Lifebuoy". Another story told by Stanley to Jack was when Stanley first started working in the shop as an apprentice when the shop had only recently been put on electricity. This new-fangled power prompted this 'jolly jape': Ray's had a huge coffee-grinder which included a large fly-wheel which was visible to the public. The handle which operated the machine was out of sight behind the counter. Young Stanley, with the connivance of another member of staff, used to kid customers that this coffee-grinder was worked by electricity!! Stan would crouch down behind the counter, from where he could just reach the wheel and his accomplice would perform some flamboyant rigmarole by calling out "switch on main switch! start motor!" etc and the hidden operator would turn the wheel making the fly-wheel revolve and dumbfounding the customer, as few people had any knowledge of the new power and saw such things as 'minor miracles'. Jack also remembers that the Double Gloucester cheeses had to be 'turned and polished' every three months. He mentions that Stanley was also proud to state that "in the fierce competition for the contract to supply The Workhouse Institute (Stow Lodge Hospital) they had beaten the Co-op."

Elsie Caroline Ray

'Toni' Ray

The Bury Street shop in the 1950's

Arthur Stanley Ray wearing Masonic regalia in the late 1920's

In his bachelor days Stanley would often take winter holidays abroad and was a keen ice-figure skater, being the only person allowed to test the ice on the pond at Abbot's Hall, before anyone else could skate on it. He was also a Freemason of the Phoenix Lodge who went through to Chapter twice; he served as Chairman of Stowmarket Town Council in 1958-59. Other interests included swimming and diving as well as being a leading member at the Rookery Bowls Club. He was also keen on sailing and would often set sail with his great friend Percy **Tydeman**. Stanley was very well-known locally for his 'fine tenor' singing voice and had been trained as a tenor by Mr **Hockey** of Ipswich. Stanley took the lead in many **Gilbert** and **Sullivan** productions around Ipswich and elsewhere in East Anglia and was soloist for many performances of oratorios in various churches and was a member of the Stowmarket Congregational Church Choir.

George Frederick **Ray**, grocer, died at the Freemasons' Hospital in Fulham on September 29th 1933, aged seventy four and was buried at Stowmarket on October 3rd. The running of the business passed to his eldest son Arthur Stanley. Kate Ellen **Ray** died at St Ives, 5 Temple Road, Stowmarket, April 26th 1941, aged eighty one.

From a tape recording owned by Jack **Ray**, made after Stanley's retirement in 1962 at Lockington Road and which features Stanley **Ray** talking to Millie **Aldous**, the long serving manageress of **Ray's** about how things had changed over the years in the shop, Millie commented that the biggest change since the 1920's in what people bought had been "pet food, as there had been no such thing back then". Millie, born 1902, the daughter of Herbert and Millicent **Aldous**, tells how before she left school, she applied for and secured a job with the Co-operative Society. George heard of this and offered her an additional half-crown 2/6d (12½p) per week to come and work for him. Her first job as an apprentice was to work in the store-room stacking candles into pyramids of ten each. Millie soon became a 'pillar' of the firm and a friend of the family and even attended the Congregational Church with members of the family.

Brenda **Jarvis** née **Flack** left school in 1944 at the age of fourteen and started work at **Ray's** for fifteen shillings (15/-) per week under the managership of Arthur Stanley (Stanley) **Ray** and also under the direct supervision of Millie **Aldous**. Brenda, who had been asked by Mr **Ray** personally to come and work for him, remembers that Millie was well known for having won many awards in the grocery business, especially for bacon cutting. On her first day at work in the shop and for the following three weeks, Brenda was given the task of weighing the white granulated sugar, which was kept in a large

G. F. RAY & SON,

Family Grocers & Provision Merchants.

Tea and Coffee Specialists,

The Model Stores, STOWMARKET.

'Phone 6.

Buy your Coffee freshly roasted. We are the only firm in the district who roast their own Coffee on the premises.

Roasted Daily & Ground to Order

Country Orders delivered free by own Motor. Distance no object.

WE SOLICIT YOUR PATRONAGE.

WE HAVE ADVANCED!

G. F. RAY

Family Grocer,

BURY STREET, STOWMARKET.

TELEPHONE 1x4.

SPECIALIST IN

TEA, COFFEE AND COCOA AND PROVISIONS.

COCOA!! ¼-lb., **7½**d. ½-lb., **1/3** 1-lb., **2/4½**
A very high-class Dutch Cocoa specially packed for us.

COFFEE!! Always delicious because always freshly roasted and freshly ground.

TEA!! The delightful fragrance and flavour of our Blends when made according to the printed directions on each packet is unexcelled.

PROVISIONS!! Can you buy finer quality Cheese and Bacon or have it delivered in better condition (always fresh) than at RAY'S?

WE shall HOLD OUR POSITION
WITH THE AID OF YOUR VALUED SUPPORT.

BUY GOODS

Produced in your EMPIRE

Buy your EMPIRE GOODS in STOWMARKET

Buy your Empire Goods at RAY'S

We Specialize in the PRODUCE of our EMPIRE

Elmswell Bacon, Hams and Home Tried Lard.
English Chedder Cheese. Finest Leicester Cheese.
Finest Australian Butter.
Empire Teas (our own blend), 1/2 per lb. upwards.
Empire Coffee (our own roasting), 2/- per lb.
Danecroft Tomatoes (always freshly picked)
Empire Flour, "National Mark," in 7lb. Cotton Bags.
English Canned Fruit—Victoria, Red and Yellow Plums, Greengages, Damsons, Raspberries, Strawberries, Gooseberries.

Our Competition—Can you guess how many Articles produced in our Empire that we sell?

G. F. RAY & SON

PURVEYORS OF THE PRODUCE OF OUR EMPIRE,

15-19, BURY STREET, STOWMARKET.

(top l.) from 1931 Official Town Guide
(above) from page 4, Stowmarket Shopping Week, June, 11th-20th 1931

wooden chest, into blue paper bags of weights of ½lb, 1lb, 2lbs and 3lbs, as well as Demerara and soft brown moist, which were kept in separate drawers. As this was still war-time, families were rationed to half a pound of sugar per person per week; if there was no sugar, they were allowed jam. Other items stored in this manner were dried fruit, which included raisins, sultanas and currants and which were packed into folded paper with the ends tucked in. Dried apricots, prunes and mixed fruit etc., were also sold in this way. Spices, allspice and pepper were packed and sold by the ounce in twisted papers. Tea that was blended on the premises by Mr Fred **Robinson**, who was also the van driver, was weighed and packed into ¼ and ½lb bags and the ends stuck with gum with the blend such as Earl Grey or Darjeeling etc. being written on thc bottom. Coffee, including Kenyan and Columbian, was blended and roasted at the rear of the shop and ground in full view of the customers. This process was carried out once a week and done on a gas-burner with the beans being turned in a cylinder. The art of getting the strength of taste just right was in the timing rather than the temperature. After this process the beans would then be blended before being ground. It was the aroma from this process for which **Ray's** shop is mostly remembered by its clientele. Coffee was parcelled up and tied with string. Various pulses (dried beans etc) including haricot, butter and black beans, split peas, marrowfat peas and lentils, all helped to extend the rations that were allowed for war-time meals. Tinned foods of fruit, vegetables, beans and soups were available as well as tins of salmon and hake. There was also a good range of dairy products such as butter, margarine and lard, Condensed Milk and Carnation Evaporated Milk and cheeses on the rind that were stored in the cellar for freshness. Whole cheeses were cut

Courtesy,
Prompt
Attention.
Your
Groceries

RAY'S

FOR

Quality,
Competitive
Prices.
Your
Provisions.

WE SOLICIT YOUR PATRONAGE

G. F. Ray & Son

15-19 Bury Street

Stowmarket

'Phone No. 6

into thirds and brought up into the shop by Mr Nelson **Wright**, where they would be cut into smaller segments, the maximum allowance during the rationing being 2oz per family. **Ray's** were renowned for their window-dressing of huge pyramids of tinned products. The shop staff were always required to wear long white starched aprons and coats. Famous brands such as Epicure, **Heinz** and **Libby's** graced these windows, with Miss **Aldous** being the window-dresser. Brown sauce, pickles and Gentleman's Relish were also available on the shelves. A limited range of biscuits was available at that time, with plainer biscuits such as Rich Tea, but also 'broken biscuits' at a slightly reduced price per pound; a few chocolate biscuits were available for those customers who could afford them and as rationing coupons would allow, eight for half a pound and sixteen for a pound. All biscuits were sold loose and then weighed into paper bags. Dried goods such as flour and oatmeal were also sold for housewives to do home-baking. Sweets were in short supply at that time, although Brenda remembers that there were generally only ever three large jars on the counter and a limited number of bars of chocolate. Cleaning products were also sold in smaller quantities: Persil, Rinso and Oxydol washing powder, Lux soap flakes, Fairy, Lifebuoy and Sunlight kitchen soap, Vim scouring powder and white candles that were sold by the pound and wrapped in newspaper to take away. The highlight of the year was when the 'first crop' of 'Danecroft Tomatoes' from the Danecroft Nursery in Finborough Road was available.

The system for the deliveries of groceries was completely different to that of modern times. It was another of Brenda's morning tasks to cycle around the town to collect the order for the weekly grocery delivery. Her varied routine covered the whole of Stowmarket with a different round each day: Monday – Chilton Avenue and Finborough Road; Tuesday (early closing day) – Ipswich Street, Lime Tree Place and Bridge Street; Wednesday – Stricklands Road, Temple Road and Unity Road; Thursday – Regent Street, Bond Street, Stowupland Street and Cardinals Road; Friday – Beech Terrace, Violet Hill, and Bury Road. It was normal sales policy for Brenda to try to promote 'Special Offers' while taking these orders to encourage people to buy extra items, which was obviously good for business. After the order books were handed in, the orders were made up for the end of week delivery which were then taken round on the trade-bike by Nelson **Wright**. Orders from people in the country were taken by telephone at the shop and were delivered in the van by Mr Fred **Robinson**. Other staff remembered by Brenda are Miss **Welham**, June **Wilden**, Mary **Messinger**, Ivor **Messinger**, Harry **Scarff** and Bert **Tyte**.

Arthur Stanley Ray circa 1960

Stan enjoying a cup of tea at Lockington Road with daughter Beryl

Arthur Stanley 'Stan' and Evelyn Mary 'Toni' Ray enjoying a holiday in the early 1960's

40 NEWBYS STOWMARKET ANNUAL, 1955.

G. F. RAY & SON LTD.

Family Grocers and Provision Merchants

The Tea and Coffee Specialists

15 & 19 BURY ST., STOWMARKET

Telephone No. 6

OUR AIM is to give you INDIVIDUAL SERVICE, COURTESY and PROMPT ATTENTION, combined with BEST QUALITY GOODS, at COMPETITIVE PRICES

Ray's entry in Newbys 1955 Stowmarket Annual

Bert **Tyte**, who started in 1938 at the age of fourteen and a half as an apprentice working mostly as a warehouseman, remembers his duties at first involved weighing sugar etc. and general work such as checking 'goods inwards' ready for shop displays and occasionally serving in the shop. He left in 1941 to take up his call to arms during the War and returned to the shop in 1947 where he obtained the post of senior assistant. He says that all of the staff had to supply their own set of three aprons and two short white coats. The aprons were triangular in shape and were tied round the waist and the narrow part of the triangular flap was then pulled up and buttoned on to a shirt button. Staff also had to arrange their own laundering of their work gear, but they could wear a 'sack apron' which would protect the white coats when involved with any dirty work in the warehouse or cellars etc.

Bert also recalls that whole Stilton cheeses were bought in August, delivered with six to a crate and wrapped in straw and stored in the cellar where they would be 'turned' every week and regularly tested with a taster which took a sample to check whether they would be ripe and ready for Christmas. Whole cheeses weighing between forty to fifty pounds had to have their rinds removed and were popular with farmers especially at harvest time.

Arthur Stanley Ray pictured with daughter Evelyn Beryl (Beryl) in Lockington Road

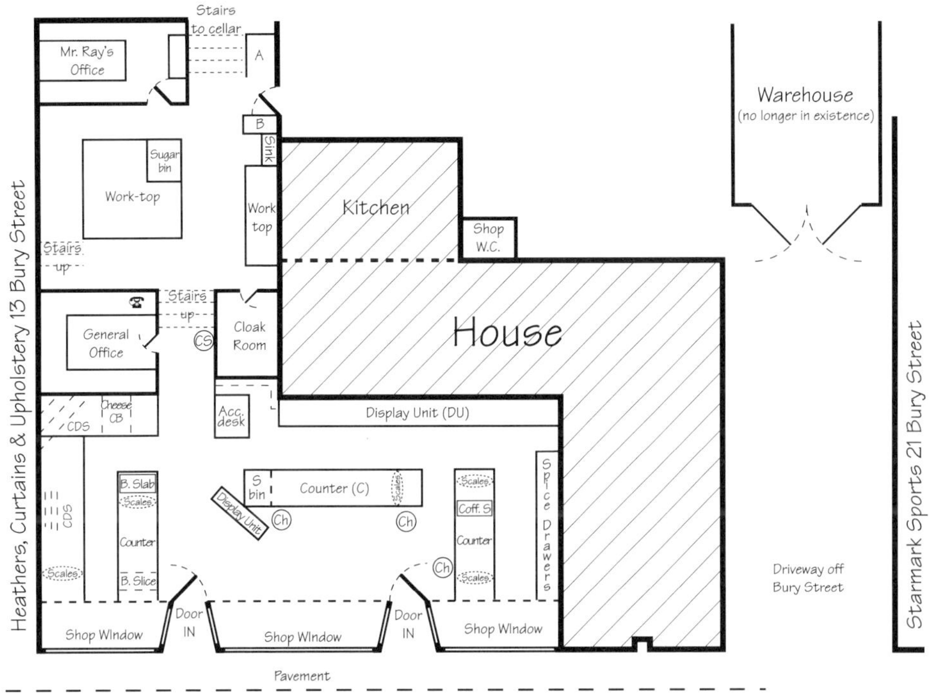

KEY

A. =	Carton Store	B. =	Coffee Roaster	B slab =	Butter slab
B slice =	Bacon slicer	Coff. S =	Coffee scales	C. =	Counter
Ch. =	Customers' chairs	CDS =	Cheese display shelves	Cheese CB =	Cheese cutting board
CS =	Coke stove	S. bin =	Sugar bin		

A plan of Ray's shop based on a sketch provided by Brenda and Ray Jarvis

Ward's shoe shop occupying Ray's former grocers shop in the 1970's

The cellar was at the rear of the premises and always maintained a constant temperature, ideal for many foodstuffs. Pulses etc. were stored in a small room upstairs and items that needed to be kept particularly dry, such as custard powder, were kept in a small back room downstairs. Bert believes that **Ray's** were also the first in the area to have a machine that could 'de-stone' raisins. Opening hours were in line with the rest of the town with the exception of the three to four weeks before Christmas when they closed at 10:00pm. On Saturday evenings the cleaning procedure for scrubbing the counters and washing the bacon-slicer was started at 5:00pm for the slightly earlier closing at 5:30pm, thus allowing the employees to go to the 'first house' at either of the two cinemas at that time. However, if they got what many of the staff dubbed an 'L.M.C' (last-minute-customer), they had to serve him with a courteous smile and start the cleaning procedure over again.

'Toni' died in February 1966 and Stanley died at their house 'Martinhoe' in Lockington Road in March 1967. After the closure of the store in 1968, the premises were occupied for some time from the mid 1970's by **Ward's** shoe shop. The site is currently occupied by Stowmarket Studios, photographic studio and Marilyn's (ladies' lingerie). ❑

Revett's

MOTOR-CYCLE DEALERS & REPAIRERS

Many people will remember **Revett's** the motorcycle shop at the top end of Ipswich Street, which carried on a brisk trade from the mid 1950's for thirty-seven years during a very popular period of interest in many aspects of motorcycling. Geoff **Revett** of Ipswich who had made his name as a motorcycle and scramble star opened the Stowmarket shop in 1955. However, the name of **Revett** was already well established in that field with its base firmly rooted in Ipswich.

The first **Revett's** was opened as a cycle agency in Berners Street, Ipswich, by twenty-three year old Valentine Henry (Val) **Revett** at the end of 1907 and the first entry in the first account book is dated January 1908. Val had been born in Ipswich on February 14th (Valentine's Day) 1884, the son of Francis and Ellen **Revett** and the 1901 Census lists the family at 1, Beck Street, Ipswich with Francis aged fifty-two, a house painter; his wife, Ellen, aged fifty-one; Valentine, son, aged seventeen, a stationer's packer; May, daughter, aged fourteen, a boot-trade fitter; Arthur, nephew, aged eighteen, boot-trade clicker, all born in Ipswich and Louisa **Smith**, mother-in-law, aged seventy-seven, born at Framlingham.

From research carried out by John F. **Bridges** in his book *'Early Country Motoring (Cars and Motorcycles in Suffolk 1896 – 1940)'* it is explained that in 1905 Val started working at 6 – 8 St Nicholas Street in Ipswich for his brother-in-law, Charles **Hammond**, who had produced his own bicycle called the 'Gainsborough' and then proceeded to build motorcycles and tri-cars using the same name. Two years later Val started his own cycle business, with limited capital, at 1 Berner Street in Ipswich and during the week he would borrow his brother-in-law's best bicycle so that he could display it in the window of his own shop. Business slowly picked up so that by 1912 they were in a position to open another cycle shop in St. Matthew's Street. It was after the First World War that Val took the decision to launch into the rapidly developing motor-cycle business and in 1921 a shop was opened in Granville Street. In 1926 a garage was built at Barrack Corner catering solely for sales and repairs of motor-cycles. Val was a founder member of the Bicycle Club and Motor-Cycle Club and also chairman of the 'The Ipswich Red Triangle Club' (founded 1925). Val and his two eldest sons often competed in many motor-cycle events but it was Val's son, Geoff **Revett**, born November 1919, whose name became known locally as an accomplished scrambler. Geoff joined the family business in 1934 and his first machine, bought for 10/- (50p), was an 'Alldays', which he pushed to Akenham to try out by driving round a farmer's field. Geoff married Kathleen Joy **Garnham** in Ipswich in 1947.

By 1955 Val was semi-retired, but still saw the advantage of acquiring a vacant premises in Ipswich Street, Stowmarket where a showroom and repair depot was established and managed by Geoff **Revett**. The following year an extensive industrial site was obtained on Norwich Road, Ipswich, which was developed into large showrooms and workshops

Revett's in the early days of trading. The shop was later extended into the cottage next-door (now Ladbrokes) and the Autocare Centre was established in the shop nearest the camera which was Burketts Giftware (see photograph opposite)

etc. As well as Geoff being in charge of the works and sales department of the family business, there were also three of his brothers involved: Francis (Frank) ran the Offices and Administrative side of the business and Raymond (Ray) looked after the bicycle and moped section with brother Edward. In 1962 they moved into new premises at 53-67 Norwich Road, Ipswich. The three-storey building's facilities contained the most modern workshop and showroom in East Anglia. Geoff then devoted his time to the new Ipswich premises, leaving the Stowmarket shop in the capable hands of Bill **Calver**, with Geoff calling in every Wednesday to maintain the family connection. The Stowmarket outlet concentrated on small motorbikes and mopeds for work, as well as selling the Watsonian, Swallow and Canterbury range of sidecar outfits and Reliant three-wheeler cars, for which they had been local agents since the mid-1950's. Another long-standing member of staff from that period was Denny **Reeve**, who became manager there when Bill accepted a directorship of the company based at Ipswich. In the early to mid-sixties the big seller was the very popular Lambretta scooter, these being

Val Revett and his well-wheeled family
back row (l. to r.) Arthur, Bernard, Kathleen, Val, Ellen, Leslie, Francis
front row (l. to r.) Edward, Raymond, Geoffrey, Winifred, Nancy, Joyce

Revett's shop and their adjacent Autocare accessories centre

delivered twenty-nine at a time in a boxcar from Ipswich Station. The Japanese Honda motorbikes began to make an appearance at this time, but the British bikes such as Triumph, BSA, Vincent, AJS, Ariel and Norton (**Bolton's** of Ipswich had the agency for Sunbeam, Royal Enfield and Matchless) were still dominant up until the early 'seventies. After this period the popularity of these Japanese bikes really accelerated and manufacturers such as Yamaha, Suzuki and Kawasaki quickly replaced the older British makes, so that 1980 saw the biggest year of number of registration sales of new machines. This trend was not sustainable however and sales decreased for a decade until motor-cycling became more popular once again with the television coverage of the World Superbikes and Grand Prix races etc. Every novice was given basic instruction on motorcycle handling before they were allowed to take their machine onto the streets. This involved a few circuits around the Duke's Head car park getting used to starting and stopping, gear changing and braking etc. This later developed into a training school that involved the local council and police and was run on a voluntary basis. Students were given more advanced instruction consisting of road runs at night, two hour sessions concentrating on vehicle handling by weaving between traffic cones and a one hour accompanied run around the countryside. Only after this would they be tested by a traffic sergeant from Bury St Edmunds who would judge their proficiency and ability to apply to take their full-licence motorcycle test.

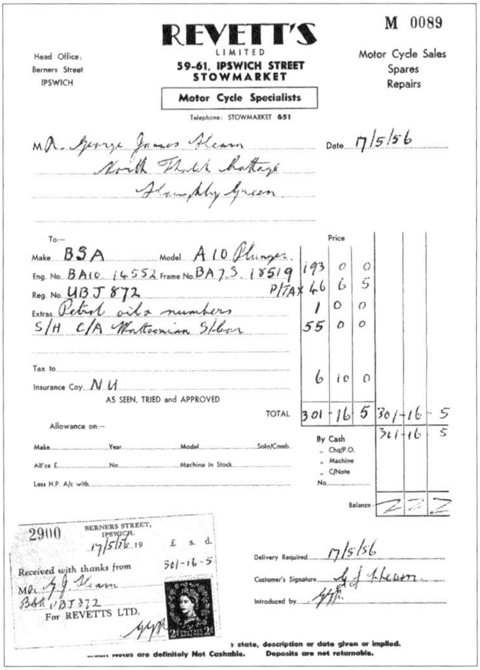
REVETT'S LIMITED
M 0089
Head Office: Berners Street IPSWICH
59-61, IPSWICH STREET STOWMARKET
Motor Cycle Specialists
Telephone: STOWMARKET 651
Motor Cycle Sales Spares Repairs
Mr. George James Hearn
North Thatch Cottage
[illegible] Green
Date 17/5/56
Make BSA Model A10 Plunger
Eng. No. BA10 14552 Frame No. BA7S 18519 — 193 0 0
Reg. No. UBJ 872 — P/TAX 46 6 5
Extras Petrol oil & numbers — 1 0 0
S/H C/A [illegible] — 55 0 0
Tax to — 6 10 0
Insurance Coy. N U
AS SEEN, TRIED and APPROVED
TOTAL 301 16 5
By Cash 301 16 5
Delivery Required 17/5/56
Received with thanks from Mr. G. J. Hearn, BSA UBJ 872, 301-16-5
For REVETTS LTD.
... state, description or date given or implied. ... Notes are definitely Not Cashable. Deposits are not returnable.

A sales invoice from 1956

Although not an absolutely necessary requirement for a job at **Revett's**, it is acknowledged that everyone who worked there was an enthusiast and many would be involved with scrambling at all the local meetings such as Shrubland Park, Raydon, Great Bentley, Eye, Bramford and Creeting Sand Pits in Suffolk and also Little Loveney Hall at Wakes Colne and Gosfield in Essex. Geoff **Revett** excelled in all forms of motorcycle riding as well as scrambling. He rode for Norwich City at Speedway events and the '**Revett** Straight' at the Snetterton Race Track was named after him. Geoff negotiated many of his business deals at such meetings and his van and bikes on the trailer were their own advertisements. At one such meeting Geoff helped out a fellow competitor, a complete stranger, by paying for a wrecked engine to be replaced so that he could continue racing.

Bill **Calver** started work for **Revett's** in Berner Street, Ipswich, but in 1954 was asked to help prepare premises in Stowmarket in readiness for opening up a motorcycle sales and repair shop in August the following year. The premises had formerly been two old cottages numbered 63 and 65 Ipswich Street, being sandwiched between **Cole's** furniture store and The Giftware shop that had once been the studio and shop for local photographer Doris **Francis**. Bill, who started at the shop as a salesman before becoming manager, describes the late 'fifties and early 'sixties as being the "halcyon days" of the business: the Lambretta scooters and NSU 'Quickly' mopeds having developed a mass appeal amongst the younger generation. The shop opening hours were 8:00am to 6:00pm for the first few years, later changing to 8:30am to 5:30pm, but Bill was always there at least a half an hour before the shop opened and was always proud of the friendliness and helpful service that they were able to provide.

An early photograph of members of the Stowmarket & District Motor Cycle & Light Car Club

It was Bill and Geoff who inaugurated Stowmarket Motorcycle and Light Car Club to promote enjoyment and companionship amongst its members. The club would also get together at Christmas time to collect and distribute groceries and other seasonal fare on their motorcycles to local pensioners. Bill remembers the successful inclusion of the Reliant three-wheeler into the shop's stock during the mid 'sixties, when the sales at Stowmarket exceeded those of the Ipswich branch. The three-wheeler's appeal was attributed to the fact that they could be driven on a motorcycle licence and had extremely low fuel consumption, thus being cheap motoring. To accommodate the growing demand for motorcycle accessories, **Revett's** acquired the adjacent premises (ex-Doris **Francis**' studios) for storage and sales: panniers, spotlights, crash-bars, helmets, gauntlets and boots etc. being the main items sold. Bill also mentions his great respect for Geoff for his abilities in dealing with every kind of problem that arose with either staff or equipment in a calm and efficient manner and he considered him to be "one of the best." He also says that Geoff was renowned for his 'mad-cap antics' and humour and had a 'tomboy, devil-may-care attitude to life.' Bill and Geoff competed together in many scramble events around East Anglia and Bill says that it certainly wasn't for the prize money, which was normally five pounds, whereas the entry fee was four pounds ten shillings. It was known that scrambling was a dangerous sport and many of the **Revett's** staff who competed in such

Lambrettas outside the shop in the early 1960's

Parcels of Christmas groceries ready for delivery to local pensioners

events frequently had accidents resulting in broken bones. However, very few workdays would be lost as such was their keenness that they would appear for work in plaster after only a few days off. Bill says that after fracturing a bone in his spine he was back in the shop after only four days, despite being bound up in an iron corset. Bill left the Stowmarket shop in February 1971 and went to the Norwich Road premises in Ipswich as a Director, later becoming joint Managing Director, the only non-family member on the Board of Directors. He retired from the company in February 1988.

Dennis (Denny) **Reeve** also started at Stowmarket the same time as Bill, a month before the shop opened. Denny was involved with setting up the workshop and positioning heavy equipment such as the welder and tool racks etc. and bolting down the hydraulic ramps and the grindstone to the floor. He also remembers installing an old Morrison air-raid shelter as a workbench that was to become a permanent feature. In the year that the Stowmarket shop opened, a Matchless motorcycle could be purchased for £105. Denny was also a well-known scrambler who competed on the local circuits and mentions the Boxing Day Trials that were started up in 1958 and were a light-hearted affair, carried out with all the entrants wearing fancy dress. The racing on these days was not taken quite so seriously and was finished as quickly as possible, so that they could then get on with the serious business of meeting up at the Bucklesham 'Shannon' public house. When Derek **Estlea** joined **Revett's** from **Barnard's** in 1957, he remembers it as being a very busy but also a very happy workplace. He remembers selling his first BSA motorcycle for £160. Denny and Derek recalled the days when they would compete against each other

Denny Reeve in the pits at an Essex and Suffolk Border Club grass-track sramble at Bentley in 1959

in assembling the Lambretta scooters after they arrived from the station in their crates. As their skills and mechanical know-how were evenly matched, they could both complete a scooter in half an hour. Derek left in 1968 to set up his own motorcycle business in Ipswich. After the Stowmarket Carnival and Trade Fair was commenced following the Queen's visit in 1961, **Revett's** was well represented on an annual basis with a large static display and also used to exhibit at many of the Wattisham RAF Airfield open days. Denny retired in 1991 after thirty-six years in the business

Reliant 3-wheelers

Barry **Shaw** remembers coming to work at the Stowmarket shop for a few months in 1956 as a temporary replacement for Bill **Calver** who had broken his back in a motorbike accident. Barry had joined **Revett's** as a 'boy' in 1951 at the Clarkson Street premises and remembers trying to be first out to serve Val **Revett** when he called for petrol, as he always gave a sixpenny tip to whichever boy served him. After his National Service, from 1953 to 1955, he rejoined the company at the Berner Street garage where he returned after his brief stay at Stowmarket and where he stayed until 1958.

Cyril **Horrex** joined the company at Stowmarket in 1958 staying for about four years working mainly as a clerk, but also being required to assist in the stores and serving during busy times such as Saturdays. He describes this period as having a 'fabulous trade on Saturdays,' with three full time assistants on sales all day despite the fact that the ICI factory had made many people redundant around that time. Cyril mentioned the small 'Corgi' motorbikes which were developed from wartime parachutists' equipment. He also mentions Solex-Cyclemaster motorised bicycles as well as Velocettes and Puch mopeds.

SCOOTER - MOTORCYCLE - THREEWHEELER SPECIALISTS

Buy from the Leading Dealers in the Eastern Counties

REVETTS

OF

IPSWICH AND STOWMARKET, SUFFOLK

ALL THE BEST MAKES — REAL AFTER SALES SERVICE
QUALITY RANGE OF USED MACHINES
HIRE PURCHASE — EXCHANGES — INSURANCE
SPARES SERVICE BY RETURN OF POST
TYRES — BATTERIES — FAIRINGS — **CLOTHING** — **ETC.**

WE WANT YOUR BUSINESS TRY US

'Phone: IPSWICH 53726 STOWMARKET 651

Advertisement from the Eastern Counties Gazette 1963

Brian **Chilvers** started work for **Revett's** in 1960, having served in the Royal Marines until the previous year and was offered a job by Geoff **Revett**, one of the reasons being that at that time Brian owned an Ariel 350 twin motorcycle. Brian describes himself as being a 'Jack-of-all-trades' as his work was a combination of working in the stores, deliveries, collections and attending to the customers' general needs. One of his furthest deliveries was to take a motorbike on a sidecar to Beck Row near Mildenhall, a round trip of about sixty miles. People might remember Brian in the workshop, as he was the only member of staff who wore a white jacket. Brian was also involved with teaching new learner drivers the rudiments of motorcycling and says that most of this took place in the Stricklands Road, Unity Road and Temple Road area of town. He also was responsible for ensuring that Geoff's vehicle always had a full tank of petrol. Damaged motorbikes were stored at the back of the site while they awaited the insurance assessor; once this was done, most repairs were done by Denny **Reeve**, although dented panels and farings etc., were sent to **Pike's** garage for panel-beating and paintwork restoration. Brian often used to have to collect motorcycles and outstanding deliveries from the Ipswich branch using a Morris pick-up-truck. Initially he was travelling to work on his Bianci moped, but later the firm provided him with a BSA Bantam for this purpose. Brian very proudly states that he was the owner of only the second Reliant three-wheeler car to be sold from **Revett's** shop. Brian recalls an amusing tale of when the showroom was being refurbished, a new 'posh' combination went through the plate-glass window and Geoff **Revett** had a near miss as he stood by the stairs when three BSA's were pushed over and toppled 'like dominoes.' With the advent of Honda motorcycles, Brian says that they arrived in crates of three from **Davy** Brothers of Ipswich and had to be assembled at the Stowmarket shop. This involved tightening up nuts and bolts and fitting each machine with a battery etc. and then making sure everything worked.

Vera **Hearn** (née **Battle)** had from an early age been interested in motorbikes and vowed never to work in an office. Her first job was at **Page's** garage in Combs Lane, but in 1968 her talents were spotted by Geoff **Revett** who asked her to start work at the Stowmarket shop. Her first duties she describes as being general stores assistant, but when Bill **Calver** transferred to the Ipswich shop in 1971, then Vera became stores manager. At about this time the stores, which had been upstairs, were resited on the ground floor (currently Ladbroke's premises) and car parts and accessories such as spray paint, fan-belts, filters and polishes etc., were introduced to counter the falling

Her Majesty the Queen passing Revett's during a visit to the town in 1961

trade in British motorbike spares. Vera remembers helping to assemble the various makes of motorcycles and mopeds that arrived in crates at the shop. She also recalls when the laws were changed to accommodate moped designs where the machine, although keeping under the 50cc engine capacity, no longer had pedals and a restriction was placed on their speed. In addition to this in June 1973 an unpopular law was passed whereby it became compulsory to wear a crash helmet. Two extensions were built at the back of the premises to cater for the growing stock and workshop space, but when Motorspares opened in Ipswich Street in 1987 this adversely affected certain aspects of their trade. It was decided to down-scale part of the premises by moving the stores upstairs again and leasing half of the premises to Ladbrokes Betting Shop chain together with the flat above. In 1992, when the Stowmarket branch faced closure, Vera was offered a position in the Ipswich store but declined, having decided to start her own business with Darren **Wnukoski**. The venture was named Motor Cycle Technics and continued in the same field by dealing with motorcycle services, repairs and MOT's. After temporary premises in the old stores in **Thurlow Nunn's** yard in Bury Street and an outlet on Tomo Business Park in Creeting Road, the business now has permanent premises in Stowupland Street.

Eddie **Cordle** remembers, when he was a young lad in short trousers, going with his parents, who were keen followers of Motor Cycle Sports, to see Geoff **Revett**, Bill **Calver** and Denny **Reeve** competing very successfully in scrambles etc., and hoping one day that

A Revett's display under canvas in the early 1960's - thought to be at the Suffolk Show. Centre stage is the Lambretta scooter. The motor-cycle on the extreme right is an Ariel Leader and the small machine in the front is probably an NSU Quickly.

A programme from a Revett's sponsored race day at Snetterton, Norfolk in 1979

he could do the same. Eddie joined **Revett's** of Stowmarket from their Ipswich branch in 1963 and says that he had a very happy eighteen months at Stowmarket where he was encouraged by Geoff, Bill and Denny, his schoolboy heroes, to compete in Motor Cycle sports. He states with gratitude that without their help and support he would not have achieved his six Eastern Centre and nine Norfolk and Suffolk Trials Championships. Eddie was a mechanic and van driver and used to collect motorcycles for repair and sales but was eventually enticed away by a factory contract with **James** Motor Cycles, another dealer in Ipswich, before starting up his own business in 1965.

Robin **Cowling** started in **Revett's** workshop as an apprentice in June 1963 and amongst other duties he helped Derek **Estlea** to build motor-cycle wheels. On one occasion when he was asked to test-ride a 500cc Velo motorcycle, he took the 'bike along the then A45 from Stowmarket to Needham Market. Unfortunately he did not slow down sufficiently on Badley Hill as he entered the 30 mph speed limit and was caught speeding by a vigilant policeman near Freehold Road. Robin remembers that the fine was £8.00, being exactly that year's Christmas Bonus, less income tax. Robin left **Revett's** of Stowmarket in November 1966 and worked for **Cox** Motorcycles of Ipswich for eleven years. In 1977 he took over Derek **Estlea's** established business, Queensway Motorcycles off Nacton Road, Ipswich, where he was able to catch most of the passing trade for small mopeds and motorcycles where the owners worked at **Reavell's** and **Ransomes Sims** and **Jefferies**.

Revetts Motor Cycles

Synonymous with Service

59-65 Ipswich Street, Stowmarket
Telephone: Stowmarket 612651

For your Honda, Yamaha, and N.V.T. machines and Reliant Three Wheeler

We cater for the Sports rider and the Every Day machine to Commute.

Call and have a chat with our sales staff. Arrange for a Demonstration.

Shop Hours 8.30 - 5.30 Closed All Day Tuesday

Full range of
Car Accessories
Specialists in
Oil Filters
and Light Bulbs

Spares
Repairs
Accessories

H.P. Terms and
Insurance for
New or Secondhand
Arranged in
Confidence

Catalogues by request

Immediate Delivery

✶ Visit our Showroom and Accessory Department ✶

1982 advertisement

Geoff **Revett's** two sons, Christopher (Chris), born 1952 and Jeremy (Jerry), born 1955, were both involved with the company. Chris did his apprenticeship with **Henley's** of

Geoffrey Robinson and Paul Hockley in the Stowmarket workshop in the early 1980's

Ipswich and became more involved with the sales side rather than the mechanical aspect of the business. Chris, who also raced, went on to become Managing Director of the business based at Ipswich after Geoff retired. Jerry started his career at Stowmarket in September 1970. He had spent part of his school summer holidays helping in the workshops and convinced his father that he would like to start work there properly.

Although not an official apprenticeship, Jerry trained under the watchful eye of Denny **Reeve**, who was the workshop manager at the time. He taught Jerry a lot of skills over the next few years, although Jerry believes that Denny considered him to be 'hard work' at times. During this same time Jerry took up Road Racing which he enjoyed for seven seasons and attained an International home licence and in 1976 also competed in the Manx G.P races on the Isle of Man which was the amateur event run on the famous TT course. The following year Jerry decided to stop racing to concentrate on the business, which was picking up again after a lean period and he describes 1980 as being the best year of sales of motorcycles nationally since the 1960's. The shop flourished, selling the usual Japanese brands of motorcycle and Reliant three-wheeler cars, which were very popular with customers who started on small motorcycles, then sidecar outfits and never had to bother with the more involved car-test. During this peak time Jerry says that they often had between thirty and forty new models in the showroom and often used to winch some of them to the upstairs rooms.

Jerry remembers that one of the big changes came about when the town was by-passed. He states that the main A45 traffic had to come

Vera Hearn, Zia Giffkins and Carol Rowe in the stores in the early 1980's

Denny Reeve in the showroom in the 1980's

(l. to r.) Vera Hearn, David Wilson, Denny Reeve, Sean Stone and Jerry Revett

Kim Staff on her last day

Retirement presentation to Denny Reeve (l. to r.) Robert Bowyer, Sean Stone, Vera Hearn, Denny Reeve, Ann Gray, Edna Farrow, Jerry Revett and Darren Wnukoski

right through the town and they often had to stop the traffic if they wanted to get a vehicle out of the showroom, as there was no back entrance to the premises. Less traffic in the town and changes in transport choice for local workers from the I.C.I and S.I.F works etc. meant that motorcycle and moped commuting, once very popular, were becoming a thing of the past. Jerry says that unfortunately these and other factors brought about the shop closure in 1992 bringing an end to an era. Jerry went to work at the Ipswich shop until that finally closed in 2001. Jerry comments 'It was a sad time, but there was no choice and so the **Revett's** motorcycle story came to a close'. ❑

CHEMISTS

Stearn's

The building in the Market Place currently occupied by the Digital Phone Company's shop will, for a great many people in the town, always be remembered as **Stearn's** the chemists. The business, however, appears to have been founded in 1833 by Thomas **Simpson** and continued through two generations until 1910, a period lasting seventy-seven years. The **Stearn** brothers, by comparison, were only in residence for a relatively short space of time. An early Pigot's Directory of Stowmarket dated 1837 list two chemists in the town: James Bray **Cutting**, Market Place and Thomas **Simpson**, Bury Street, formerly **Fidler's** Menswear, currently **Tydeman's** Jewellers. Thomas **Simpson**, son of George **Simpson**, married Charlotte Sophia **Freeman**, daughter of Lankaster **Freeman**, on 27th September 1839 in Stowmarket. The two chemist shops continued for several years, but by 1855 a Mr William **Jackson** was dispensing at the Market Place shop and Mr **Simpson's** address was given as Tavern Street. Thomas **Simpson**, who had been born in Stonham Aspall on 22nd March 1800, died 6th January 1873 aged seventy-two. The 1873 Kelly's Directory shows that the executors of Thomas **Simpson's** will were druggist and chemist in the Market Place, along with a Mr Charles **Suttle**. The 1881 Census shows the **Simpson** family living in Station Road, with Charlotte, widow aged sixty-six born at Rattlesden, chemist shop proprietor, Thomas, son, thirty-seven, banker's clerk, Charlotte, thirty-four, Charles, thirty-three, auctioneer's man, Robert, twenty-nine, chemist and druggist and Sarah, twenty-five, all children of Thomas and Charlotte, born in Stowmarket. Also included in that list were Henry aged four, a nephew, Albert **Elston**, eighteen, chemist's assistant born Deeping St James, Lincolnshire, servants Jane **Sheering**, eighteen and Emma **Tricker**, thirty-four, both born in Leiston and Eliza **Kerry**, fourteen, born Stowupland. Next door lived Mr Spencer **Freeman** aged seventy-six, retired surgeon and registrar and also a well-known local personality. By 1885 the executors of Thomas **Simpson** & Son were listed as chemists, druggists and agents to the Sun and the Union Insurance Companies and depot for the British and Foreign Bible Society, Market Place. From 1888 to 1892 they also had a shop in Bury Street, listed as dispensing family and agricultural chemists and druggists. The 1891 census shows Charlotte, now retired and son Robert, manager of the premises, helped by assistant chemist Henry **O'Neal**, aged twenty-five, from Winslow in Buckinghamshire and

Thomas Simpson's chemist shop from an early coloured postcard

Ernest P Simpson dispensing in a room behind the shop

apprentice Harry **Boby**, aged seventeen, from Bacton. (Harry Rowland **Boby** and later his son, George, were to be the unifying link through the coming years by working for **Simpson, Stearn, Simkin** and **Flett**) Thomas **Simpson**, the son of Charlotte, was only a few doors away as manager of the bank that was later to become **Hayward's** solicitors. Charlotte **Simpson**, who had been born 10th October 1814, died at 5 Market Place on 27th March 1895 aged eighty years.

The **Stearn** family was living at Sheepcote Hall, Stowupland where Leonard was born 13th June 1873 and Sydney was born 9th March 1875, two of the nine children of Edwin **Stearn** and Sarah (née **Pyman**). The 1881 Census shows: Edwin **Stearn**, head, aged forty-five, farmer; Sarah aged forty-seven his wife; Thomas E. aged eighteen, farmer's son; Ernest aged fifteen, farmer's son; Harry, aged fourteen, grocer's apprentice; Sarah E. aged twelve, scholar; Laura aged eleven, scholar; Roland aged nine, scholar; Leonard aged seven, scholar; Sydney aged six, scholar and Margaret aged five months. About 1910, the two brothers Leonard and Sidney took over the running of chemist shop in the Market Place that was to bear their name till 1992. The 2nd September 1911 saw the marriage of Sydney to Daisy Beatrice **Tidmarsh** at Stowmarket Parish Church. In 1912, Leonard, who remained a bachelor all his life, moved to Haverhill to set up in business there, opening his own chemist shop at 21, Queen Street. A 1933 directory shows he also had opened a shop at 268, Mill Road, Cambridge. 1933 was also the year that Leonard sold the Haverhill business to Mr Davidson Martin **Graham**, a chemist who had worked in London. Mr **Graham** remembers Mr **Stearn** as being an honest and kindly man, "one of England's gentlemen", who thought nothing of donning his knickerbockers, Norfolk jacket and cap and cycling the thirty miles to Stowmarket to see his relations. The 1916 Kelly's shows

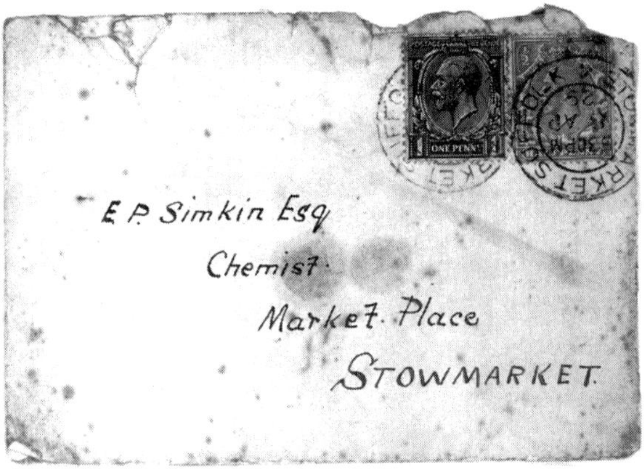

SHAKE THE BOTTLE

WILD CHERRY Cough Balsam FOR ADULTS

Tinct. Ipecac. 8·0, Emuls. Chlorof. 9·4, Liq. Morph. B.P. 2·0 v/v, Tinct. Capsici 0·3, Acetum Scillæ 20·0, Syr. Pruni Verg. 10·0, Liq. Cocci 0·3, Syr. Rib. Nig. and Syrupus ad 100·0.

CAUTION - IT IS DANGEROUS TO EXCEED THE STATED DOSE

DOSE.—Half to one tea-spoonful, three or four times a day.

E. P. SIMKIN, Ph.C., M.P.S.
Pharmaceutical Chemist
(STEARN BROS.)
STOWMARKET.
ESTABLISHED 1833 TEL. 35

BEAUFOY'S VINEGAR,

FOR PICKLING.

T. SIMPSON & SON, Chemists, &c.,
MARKET PLACE, STOWMARKET.

N.B.—Families supplied with the most approved Fish Sauces, Spices, &c., of superior quality.

ROSEMARY, QUININE, AND CANTHARIDINE HAIR WASH

For restoring and promoting the Growth of the Hair.

This preparation is strongly recommended when the Hair is weak, and a gentle stimulant required; it promotes the growth, refreshes the Skin, and is most effectual in removing Scurf, and imparting a soft and glossy appearance to the Hair.

DIRECTIONS FOR USE—With a piece of flannel or sponge well rub the Hair at the roots three or four times a week, or as often as may be necessary

STEARN BROS,
DISPENSING CHEMISTS,
STOWMARKET.

FROM

STEARN BROS., Late T. SIMPSON & SON,

Dispensing, Family and Photographic Chemists, .

Market Place, STOWMARKET.

We respectfully beg to solicit your kind patronage, and to assure you that any orders entrusted to us shall receive our very best attention.

All Drugs, Chemicals and Pharmaceutical Preparations supplied by us are guaranteed the best quality, and our prices most reasonable.

No effort is spared to meet the wishes and requirements of our customers. Any article not in stock will be procured at the shortest notice.

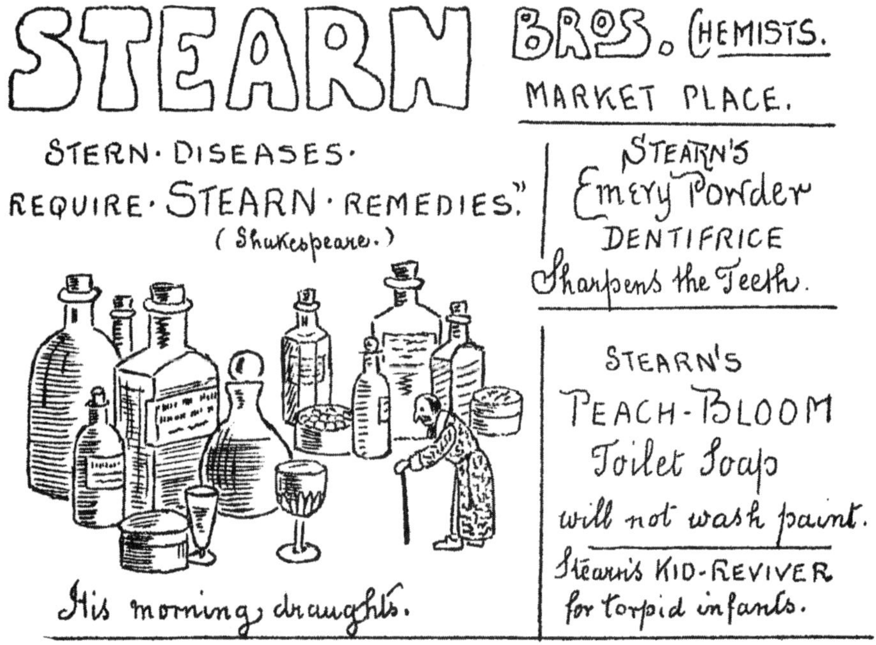

These two advertisements appeared in the (top) 1913 (no.3) and (bottom) 1914 (no.4) editions of the 'Stowmarket Dramatic Intelligencer and Trade Boomster', a hand-written, witty publication primarily about the latest productions by the Stowmarket University Extension Society Players and others which were funded by local business advertisements

the premises owned by the **Stearn** Brothers, whose entry is the same as Mr **Simpson's**, but with the addition of "dealers in photographic materials; by appointment to His Majesty the King". A 1916 rate book has Sidney **Stearn** living at 5, Market Place and he still lived and worked at the shop in 1922. In 1924 the business passed to Mr Ernest P. **Simkin**, although retaining the **Stearn** Brothers' name. Sidney **Stearn** had moved to Tuddenham Road in Ipswich and opened three more chemist shops at 159, Felixstowe Road, 90, Foxhall Road and 58, Queensway. After taking over the Stowmarket business, Mr **Simkin** was able to add "cattle and poultry medicine manufacturers" to the advertising wording with the telephone number 35.

Ernest Peach **Simkin** had been born in Rugeley in Staffordshire 11th August 1890 and learnt his trade at Southall's in Bull Street, Birmingham. Ernest had married Kathleen Clarissa **Parke** (born 19th July 1903 in Norfolk) and their son Michael was born at the Allington Nursing Home, Ipswich in 1939. Michael describes his father as being a quiet, patient and very caring man with a dry but infective sense of humour, but when the need arose he could also be strict. Ernest felt it was important to provide a real community service, and with the shop's close proximity to the Market Place he would often be called upon to treat minor cuts, splinters and remove dust and grit etc. from eyes, especially on market days. He would also provide bandages, plasters and poultices for sprains and sores. Whenever possible he would recommend natural treatments such as dock leaves, witch hazel, malt, Kaolin and Morphine, cough linctus, Calamine lotion and aspirin. Ernest's attention to detail was meticulous with the dispensary's needing to be kept well ordered and all the bottles arranged alphabetically. The large, ornate glass jars filled with various coloured liquids displayed in the windows by all chemists were visual symbols of the chemists' qualifications, the liquid having to be changed every six months to prevent fading. For some years the Royal Coat of Arms was displayed behind the large brass mortar and pestle over the shop doorway. This denoted Royal patronage for supplying **Day's** game paste to the Sandringham Estate. In 1935 Ernest had the interior of the shop completely refitted with glass-topped, wooden counters which also included a clock as well as shelving to display all the various containers for the pills and potions that they had available. At the rear of the shop was a long glass panel that enabled the dispenser to keep an eye on the shop when he was 'out the back' making up prescriptions, although there were seven other shop staff normally on hand at most times. Having been dispensed, prescriptions were wrapped and sealed with sealing wax before being handed to the customer, or delivered in the lunch hour. The brass window plates below each front window inscribed '**Stearn** Bros. Chemists' had to be cleaned every morning, weather permitting, but were removed every evening and stored in the greenhouse at the back of the premises.

Ernest, a pipe smoker, enjoyed reading and listening to the radio and was also a member of the Rookery Bowls Club. Other forms of relaxation he enjoyed included walking along stretches of the Suffolk Coast at Southwold and Walberswick as well as Scotland and Wales.

As a child brought up during the war years, Michael remembers his bedroom as consisting of a hammock in the cellar next to the coal shute and storage area for brown

The Royal Coat of Arms is currently owned by Michael Simkin

winchesters of medicines and jars of isinglass for keeping the eggs. Michael also remembers his father, who was an air raid warden, coming home and hanging his coat up behind the door with his gas mask and torch. The family's dining table at this time was a '**Morrison**' shelter, which was much used by family and friends. After the war Michael can remember being asked to help in the business by doing some of the local deliveries on a trade-bike and he comments "taking oxygen and goods up to Stow Lodge Hospital at Onehouse was a long slog". Mr Fred **Wright** was the 'general help' who did most of the deliveries.

In 1950, James Donald Munro (Don) **Flett** started work with Ernest **Simkin**. The business became a Limited Company known as **Stearn** Bros. Ltd. in 1952 when Don **Flett** went into partnership with Ernest **Simkin**.

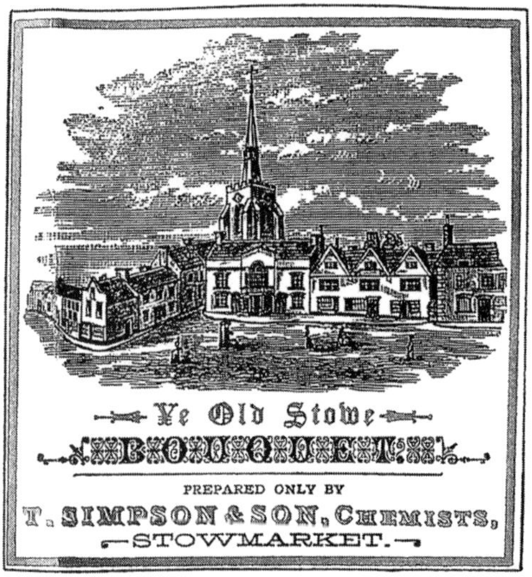

Don **Flett** was born 13th February 1916 on the Isle of Harris, Hebrides on the West Coast of Scotland. At the age of twelve, he moved with his family to Aberdeen where he continued his education. In 1934 he attended college in Aberdeen to train to become a pharmacist; he took the written papers in London and the practical examinations in Edinburgh. When he qualified in 1938, aged twenty-two, he had completed the six year course in only four years. He then started work for G. L. **Spence**, a pharmacy in Aberdeen, who held the sole agency for tubercular vaccine outside Switzerland and who, like all other chemists at that time, made their own pills. He carried out private dispensing for five nursing homes in the city and worked solely for them. In 1939, he was promoted to manager of the branch. He married Margaret **Anderson** in 1940 in Aberdeen. However, in 1941 he joined the services becoming a trainer and observer with the Royal Air Force. Having completed his training as a bomb-aimer in South Africa he returned to England in January 1943. Margaret and Don's first child, Donald Moffatt Alexander, was born in 1944. At the end of the War in 1945, Don and his family moved to Cambridgeshire where he worked for K. **Hart** (Chemist) Ltd., Newmarket Road, Cambridge. Their second child, Catherine, was born in 1946. Don stayed with **Hart's** for five years, moving to Stowmarket in 1950.

STEARN'S

WORM POWDERS

FOR PIGS.

Quickly remove all kinds of Worms and restore the Pig to perfect health.

DIRECTIONS.—To be given in a small bait of mixed food in the morning and repeated in a week if necessary. One powder is sufficient for a full-grown pig, small pigs should be given less in proportion.

Price - Per Box of 7 Powders, 1/-

PREPARED ONLY BY

STEARN BROS., Veterinary Chemists,

STOWMARKET.

SPIRIT OF TURPENTINE

STEARN BROS.

(E. P. SIMKIN, Ph.C., M.P.S.)

CHEMISTS

STOWMARKET

Estd. 1833 Tel. 35

SPIRIT OF TURPENTINE

STEARN·BROS.

DISPENSING · CHEMISTS

STOWMARKET

ESTABLISHED · 1833

HARTSHORN & OIL.

POISONOUS.—NOT TO BE TAKEN.

STEARN·BROS.

DISPENSING · CHEMISTS

STOWMARKET

ESTABLISHED · 1833

Advertisements and jar labels

Some of the ornate storage jars used by Stearn's

Joyce Clover (née Farrow) standing in front of the brass window sill which had to be taken in every night and cleaned, as it was replaced every morning

George Boby and Daphne Mayhew (?) behind the counter

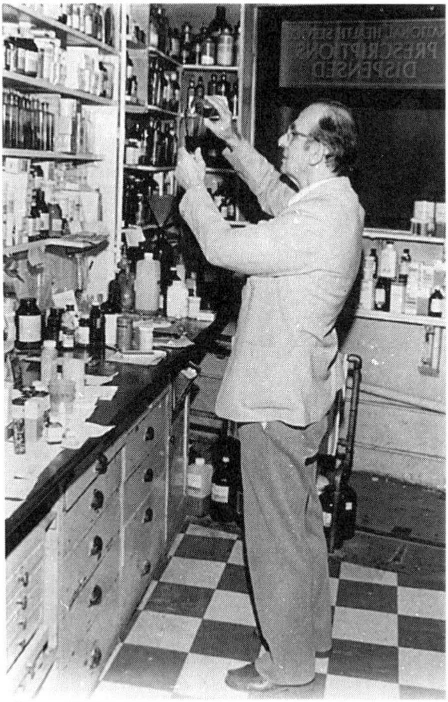

Donald Flett measuring out chemicals in his dispensary

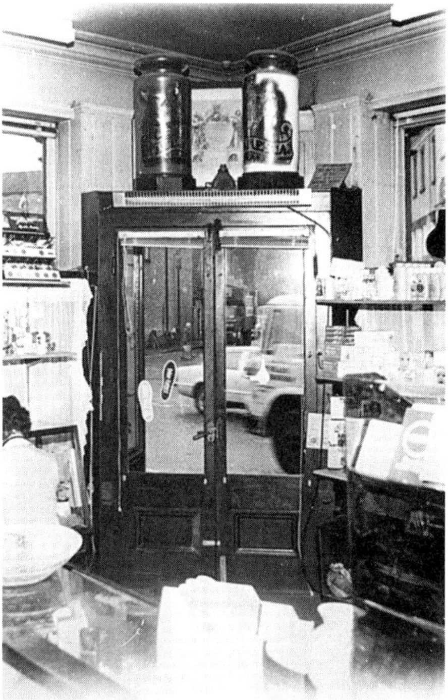

Inside the shop looking through the corner doors

Joyce Clover (née Farrow) on the steps of the large cellar under the shop, used as a store for much of the stock

A view inside the shop. Note the ornate chair provided for customers' comfort

STEARN. BROS. **THE CURE.**

Magic Corn Cure, Inc. STOWMARKET.

Dear Sirs,—For twenty years I had suffered with two severe corns. I tried numerous cures, but to no avail. Finally, a friend recommended <u>your</u> wonderful corn cure. After one application my corns were completely gone. By the way, have you anything to bring back the two toes that went with the corns ?

Sincerely, SOPHIE GLUTZ.

-Blue Gator.

STEARN BROS. LTD.
CHEMISTS
STOWMARKET
EST. 1833 Tel. 2035

ESSENCE OF PEPPERMINT

STEARN BROS.
(E. P. SIMKIN, Ph.C., M.P.S.)
CHEMISTS
STOWMARKET Tel. 35
Estd. 1833

CALAMINE LOTION
B. P. C.
E.P. SIMKIN. Ph.C., M.P.S.
(STEARN BROS.)
CHEMIST • STOWMARKET

Stearn's chemist shop a few months before its closure in 1992

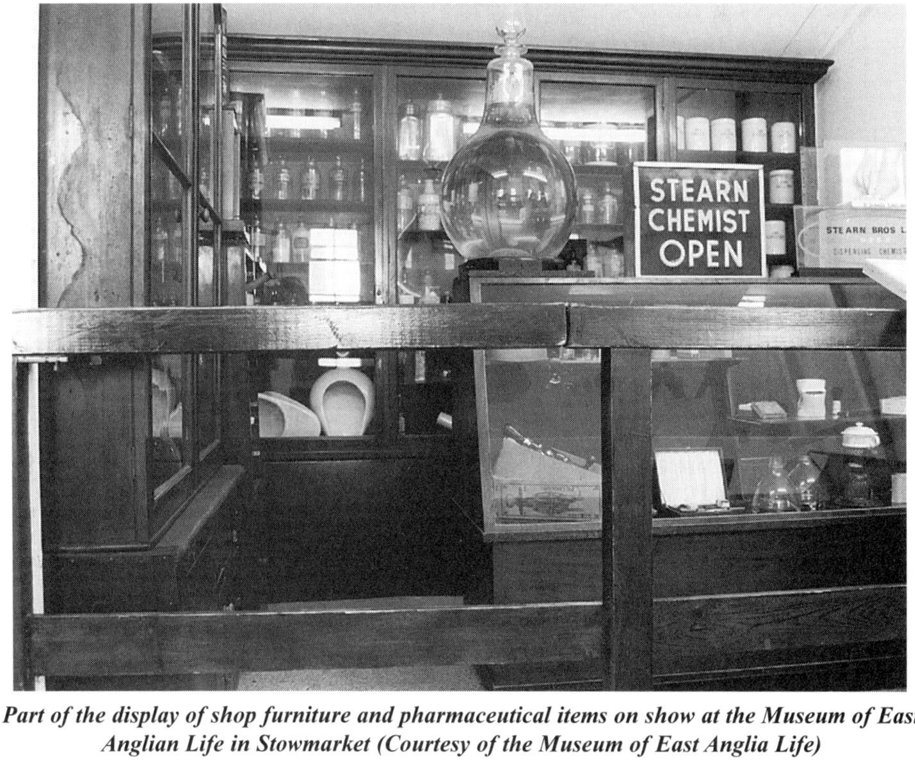

Part of the display of shop furniture and pharmaceutical items on show at the Museum of East Anglian Life in Stowmarket (Courtesy of the Museum of East Anglia Life)

Don Flett outside his shop on the day of his retirement 11th May 1992

Don explained that glass mortars were used for grinding powders and bronze ones were for general use. He graphically illustrated the reason for the different uses for the mortars by showing the authors a bronze mortar with a large hole in the side caused by an explosion as a result of a careless trainee chemist causing a spark when mixing a volatile chemical compound. After becoming a partner in 1952, Don took over the day-to-day running of the shop allowing Ernest **Simkin** to gradually reduce his commitment to the business until his retirement later that year. 1952 also saw the birth of the **Flett's** third child, Elizabeth. At this time Margaret became company secretary and went into partnership with her husband.

It was in the same year of 1952 that seventeen-year old Joyce **Farrow** was employed by the firm, initially to do labelling and packing behind the shop. She was taught the importance of never putting any liquid into an unlabelled bottle. The following recipes and remedies are a sample of the type of items packed and sold at that time: bath salts, hand lotion, chilblain ointment, carbolic oil, salts of lemon, iodine paint, sugar of lead, cough mixtures, ginger wine essence, white embrocation, tincture of myrrh, syrup of figs and senna pods. Veterinary products also stocked included: condition powder for horses and cattle, Cattle Glauber's salt, horse embrocation and John **Day's** special roup powder. After two years Joyce progressed to serving in the shop, having been trained in make-up sales, two days of this being spent on an Elizabeth **Arden** course in London. Some of the other brands of ladies' cosmetics were Yardley, Max **Factor**, Harriet **Hubbardayer**, Coty and Helena **Rubenstein**. One of Joyce's other duties was dressing the two main windows. She can also remember dealing with surgical appliances such as elastic hosiery, trusses and body belts. Joyce worked for **Stearn's** for a total of thirty-three years, having had a nine year break from 1976 - 1983 and finally leaving the business in May 1992, just two months before the shop closed its doors for the last time.

Ernest P. **Simkin** died in Stowmarket 13th March 1976, aged eighty-five and his wife, Kathleen C. **Simkin**, died in Bury St Edmunds 23rd April 1981, aged seventy-five.

In 1992, Donald **Flett** retired and sold the business. It was bought by the Boots Company and many of the old items that were in the shop are now housed in the Boots Museum in Nottingham, whilst some items are still preserved at the Museum of East Anglian Life in Stowmarket.

Donald **Flett** died in March 1998 aged eighty-two and Margaret his wife died only a few weeks later. ❑

Suffolk Iron Foundry

(Tibbenham Family)

The Industrial Revolution hit Stowmarket in the early 1800's when James **Woods** established an iron foundry in Bury Street. From Harry **Double's** 'A Book of Records' he says of James **Woods**, "A writer of the last century records that Mr James **Woods** was the first man to break in upon 'the somewhat indolent repose of Stowmarket', by establishing furnaces and forges in the Bury Street and Tavern Street area of the town". The year this account was written was 1816. However in Robert **Malster's** book on Stowmarket, he states that the foundry business had been started in 1812. The name of James **Woods**' foundry continues through many old town directories as being in Bury Street and for much of that time in competition with George **Bewley** who had premises in Crowe Street and Market Place. James had been born in Ipswich on the 24th February 1789 and had married Elizabeth at St Margaret's Church, Ipswich 18th October 1812. An 1851 census index shows James aged sixty-two, born Ipswich, living in Stowmarket with his wife Elizabeth also aged sixty-two, born Rickinghall, with children: Harriett aged twenty-seven born Buxhall, Edmund aged twenty-three, Jane aged twenty-one and Sarah aged eighteen, all born in Stowmarket. Other children not mentioned on the census include John James born 1813 at Ipswich and Elizabeth born 1815 at Buxhall. The following were all born at Stowmarket: twins Anna Maria and Laura born 1820, Susannah born 1825, William born 1828 and Louisa born 1831. Elizabeth, wife of James, died at Bury Street on June 13th 1861 aged seventy-two. In an 1868 Morris and Co's Commercial Directory and Gazetteer the entry now appears as **Woods**, **Cocksedge** and **Warner**, engineers, millwrights, iron and brass founders and agricultural implement manufacturers, Suffolk Iron Works at Market Place and at Bury St Edmunds. By 1874 it was reduced to just **Woods**, **Cocksedge** and **Co.** James **Woods** died June 8th 1877 aged eighty-eight and his son Edmund became manager of the company. J S **Cocksedge** left the partnership in about 1879. The 1881 census shows that the business was being run by Edmund **Woods**, aged fifty-seven, who is

James Woods photographed by Drazely of Stowmarket circa 1869

listed as being an engineer employing seventy-five men and fifteen boys, his wife Mary (née **Proctor**) aged forty-three born Lesbury, Northumberland and son Clement aged seventeen, an engineer with the company, Ernest aged fifteen, an engineer's clerk plus Isabella, thirteen, Fanny, twelve, Percy, eleven, Henry, ten and Frank, nine, all scholars born in Stowmarket with Mary **Diaper** aged twenty, a general servant, born Combs. In an 1885 White's Directory the company had become simply **Woods and Co** and boasted branches in Norwich, Ipswich, Newmarket and Bury St Edmunds. In an 1888 directory the entry is '**Woods** and Co engineers, manufacturers of general agricultural, hydraulic & steam machinery, millwrights, wagon & cart builders, target makers etc'. By 1910 the business had passed its peak and had developed financial problems. It was at this time that Louis **Tibbenham** was introduced as manager of the Bury Street plant.

Louis John **Tibbenham** had been born in Ipswich on September 1st 1879, son of John and Emma **Tibbenham**. He first appears on the 1881 census at 34 Carr Street, Ipswich St Margaret's. Louis's father, John, is listed as a 'Calver, builder employing three men' and aged thirty eight born Rendlesham, with Emma, wife aged forty, born Yarmouth, Norfolk, William, son aged twelve, born London, Arthur, son aged ten, born Ipswich, Frank, son aged six, born Ipswich, all

The Tibbenham family photographed in 1898
(standing l. to r.) Arthur, Frank, Louis, John (father) and Frederick
(seated l.to r.) William, Percy and Emma (mother)

scholars and Louis, son, aged two, born Ipswich, with Anna **Tibbenham** aged thirteen, a domestic servant. Additionally there had been two children who died in infancy: John 1867-68 and Sydney 1876-77. After this census, two more children were born: Frederick later in 1881 and Percy born 1884, both born in Ipswich. Louis later described himself as the 'weakling' of the six surviving brothers, who did not excel at school but who showed aptitude for technical drawing. In due course he became apprenticed to **Ransomes Sims** and **Jefferies** as a tracer and assistant draughtsman and was signed on 11th June 1894. In order to supplement his wage, he purchased Indian ink in stick form from China to sell to his fellow draughtsmen at half-a-crown (2/6d) (12½p) per stick, compared with the more normal price of 7/6d (37½p). The quality of the ink was not quite the same, but adequate.

At the end of his apprenticeship he was offered 27/6d (£1:37½ p) per week to stay on for another six weeks, but he accepted an opportunity as an engineering draughtsman at 35/- (£1:75p) per week with **Lever Bros** at Port Sunlight, where he stayed for one year and learnt skills in advertising. He then moved to **Clayton** and **Shuttleworth**, Lincoln at £1-17s-6d (£1:87½p) per week as a traction engine draughtsman. This was a ten year period, during which he secured his first house (a small terraced property at £16 per annum rental). During this period he married and produced two sons, Frank born 1907 and Don born 1910. Although gaining valuable experience, he desperately wanted to run his own business. Then in October 1910, he was offered the position of manager of **Woods** & Co., a small foundry in Bury Street, Stowmarket employing fifty people. He took over the post cold, replacing the departing manager with no introduction to the other staff or any information on the normal business procedures; he was just left to get on with it.

Louis John Tibbenham

After taking over as manager at the foundry, Louis quickly found out the trouble the company was in. He soon had assessed the problems but the old company of **Woods** & Co. went into receivership. However, Louis persuaded the liquidator to sell the freehold of the bankrupt property to George **Thurlow** who already had neighbouring property producing leather belts for agricultural machinery. From this arrangement, Louis leased the foundry from **Thurlow's** and was able to continue production of some of the machinery, including ploughshares. The business picked up and Louis floated the company and changed the name from **Woods** & Co. to the Suffolk Iron Foundry and continued at the Bury Street site throughout the First World War. However, by the end of the war, business and orders had fallen away and so the company went into receivership. In 1919, **Thurlow's** business was expanding fast and needed the extra space, so Louis was not able to renew his lease of the foundry and so had to look for new premises.

A photograph dated 1st February 1920 showing the construction of the Foundry building by Boulton & Paul (Norwich) in Prentice Road

S.I.F.

MANAGING DIRECTOR.

W. S. Cowell, Ltd., Ipswich

S.I.F.

SUFFOLK IRON FOUNDRY
(1920) LTD.

A
Smoking Concert,

ON THE OCCASION OF THE OPENING OF THE
NEW FOUNDRY,
WILL BE HELD AT THE
"KING'S HEAD" HOTEL,
SEPT. 17TH, 1920,
8 p.m.

Chair to be taken by
J. M. PRENTICE, Esq.

S.I.F.

Programme.

Song (Local)
Humorous Sketch - C. Cullingford.
"Stuttering Sammy" - J. Connell.
Song (Local)
Humorous Magic - C. Cullingford.
Selected - - - - - J. Connell.
Song (Local)
"The Vicar and I will be there"
C. Cullingford.
"Parson and me" - - J. Connell.
Song (Local)

GOD SAVE THE KING.

Pianist - - - E. BAKER.

S.I.F.

Toasts.

THE COMPANY.

EMPLOYEES.

CONTRACTORS.

CARRIERS,
G.E.R. and CARTERS.

VISITORS.

The programme for a SIF smoking concert* held to mark the opening of the new foundry
****a concert usually involving local entertainment at which smoking (euphemistically) is allowed***

Louis felt he had a very good knowledge of foundry work and had the idea that a foundry producing quality castings could supply those local engineering companies who frequently considered foundry work to be dirty and of minor importance. In the course of his discussions, he negotiated with a Chelmsford firm which later became **Crompton Parkinson**, who made electrical switchgear and machinery etc. Louis was able to supply them with electric motor end castings, the profits of which helped him finance his new venture of building a new foundry.

Louis' decision to purchase the town's 'bog', which was six acres of un-drained land near the railway station, caused amusement amongst the townsfolk who thought him slightly mad. The land, bought from Stowmarket Urban District Council, was close to where railway track and equipment had sunk from sight during the building of the Great Eastern railway in the 1840's. However, Louis was sure of his aims as he knew that all the factories in Lincoln had been built on similar bog-land by driving deep pilings.

The site was developed and became operational in 1920 and to mark the occasion a 'Smoking Concert' was held. The company became known as **Suffolk Iron Foundry (1920) Limited** with its trademark logo of **SIF** at the Gipping Works, Prentice Road and by 1925 had the telephone number of 13 Stowmarket. At about this time son Frank joined the company which had just won an award from the Foundry Trade Journal for the best design of a new foundry. However, this was soon over-shadowed by the gloom of the depression and the subsequent General Strike of 1926, which resulted in the **Crompton Parkinson** contract being nullified due to that company's merger with another company leaving SIF with no orders. This void prompted Louis to realise that to give a casting a coat of paint made it a finished product, thus generating a greater profit. The change of direction led to the production of mangles (which consisted of a large amount of cast iron framing), sports equipment such as tennis posts etc. and the simple push mower. Although orders for mangles were usually in dozens, production at the factory received an unexpected boost when, in 1932, a Mr **Kaufmann** from a London showroom placed an ultimate order for five hundred. After this deal in May 1933, Mr **Kaufmann** became a half partner in the company and became responsible for the sales side of the business. New developments in the designs for the handmowers took place at about this time, but at the start of the Second World War in 1939, domestic contracts were halted in favour of war-work including ground equipment for the Royal Air Force. Louis had met and worked with a trailer manufacturer in Dereham, which subsequently became **Crane - Fruehauf**; this liaison led to the production of bomb trolleys for the munitions business including those for the famous Dam-busters 'bouncing bomb' trolleys. Frank, who had married Margaret (Peggy) **Ewins**, daughter of Sidney and Bess **Ewins** of Banbury, Oxfordshire, eventually became director of the ever expanding **Sifbronze** arm of the business. His brother Don, who had earlier worked in journalism and advertising and had formed **Willsmore** and **Tibbenham** in Holborn Road, London then started his own company called **Tibbenham** Publicity, which was based in Norwich.

After the end of the war in 1945, the domestic side of the business gradually returned to peacetime mode, with increased orders for lawn-mowers; the petrol-driven 'Suffolk Punch' was introduced in 1954 and a newspaper article dated April 1959 features one such machine at the selling price of £38-2s-6d (£38:12½p). Before this, however, Louis **Tibbenham** retired in 1955 and sold his half of the business to the **Kaufmann** Group of Companies, which in 1967 was itself purchased by the **Qualcast** Group (a Derby foundry and lawnmower manufacturer). This company later merged with Birmingham Aluminium to form **Birmid Qualcast**, a large industrial group focused on foundry work in the Midlands. The Suffolk Iron Foundry was subsequently renamed Suffolk Lawn Mowers. The SIF logo also became synonymous with other welding and metal working industries, producing 'Sifbronze' welding rods for various types of weld etc which have become well known throughout the world and still continues today as a leader in its field. Frank retired from the company in 1974 and handed the directorship over to his son Patrick Maskell (Paddy) **Tibbenham**, who was then aged thirty-two and had joined the company two years earlier. Paddy married Mary Elizabeth **Mason** of West Bridgford, Nottingham June 2nd 1966 and had a son Mark, born May 19th 1967 and daughter Jill Elizabeth, born May 13th 1969. Mark is a Senior Operations /Database Manager of **Thompson** and **Morgan** (Young Plants) Ltd. Ipswich and is married to Irene **Francis** of Southend-on-Sea. Jill is an occupational therapist in Chester and is married to Christopher **Palin**, they have two sons Ross Thomas and Toby James.

In 1975, the old SIF foundry was closed due to insufficient throughput, many mower parts then being produced from aluminium or plastics. Additionally, the cast-iron machine shop was nearing the end of its useful life, so the decision was taken to re-design the engine, which would be based on an aluminium block. Production on the Qualcast

A Suffolk Iron Foundry lorry parked at Pike's garage, Combs Ford, in the early 1950's

A lorry full of Suffolk Punch lawnmowers passing through the town in the 1960's

The path beside the River Gipping with the Foundry building running alongside it

An inside view of the workshop in the 1920's

A coffee grinder made at the Suffolk Iron Foundry in the 1920's, currently on display in the office of Mr Paddy Tibbenham at the SIFbronze factory in Prentice Road, Stowmarket

'Concorde' range of electric motors followed in 1980. Modernisation and amalgamation then followed fairly speedily as in 1988 Birmid Qualcast was purchased by Blue Circle Industries. The Derby lawnmower site closed in 1991 and its production moved to the Stowmarket site. A management buy-out of the company from Blue Circle Industries in 1992 was followed by the takeover by Robert **Bosch** of Stuttgart in 1995. The comment is as valued today as it was in the early 1800's: that unique skills are required to produce saleable goods at reasonable prices. Technology in battery development is such that some products are now 'cordless', but the good old handmower is still in demand and made in quantity.

Paddy **Tibbenham** and his Sales Manager, John **Rose**, completed a management buy -out from Atco Qualcast in December 1994, such that SIFbronze is housed in the old SIF office block and tool room in Prentice Road. The initials SIF continue on a range of welding consumables. ❑

Turner Bros (Stowmarket) Ltd

WHOLESALE CONFECTIONERS

On the 10th October 1910 (10/10/10), Arthur **Ayling-Turner** and his wife Emily (née **Divall**) moved with his family from London to Brettenham in Suffolk. Arthur was born in Brighton, Sussex in 1873 and later became a journeyman carpenter. Emily had been a court dressmaker to Queen Alexandra, but they also ran a wet-fish business in Whittington Road, Edmonton. At some time a decision was taken to move the family to Suffolk and the journey was undertaken using a horse and cart during the course of which one of the children, Fred, broke a leg and ended up in Bury St Edmunds Hospital after spending a night at Preston (Suffolk). After their move to Suffolk, they took over the property called Water Hall, Brettenham, which was a small farm.

Their children were Arthur George (Bruv), born Brighton 1896; Emily Ruth (Cissie), born Brighton 1898; Frederick (Fred), born Edmonton 1900; Charles Edwin, born Edmonton 1902; May, born Edmonton 1905 and Elizabeth (Bessie), who was born at Brettenham in 1914. In 1918 Fred went into the army and served in the final stages of the First World War and afterwards served the remainder of his duty in India before coming back to the family business. In 1920 the family moved to Fasbourn Cottage in Buxhall from where brothers Arthur and Charles used to sell sweets, rock and confectionery from a market stall on a Saturday evening; they also used to supplement their income by travelling around selling glassware such as tall glasses to public houses etc. It was also convenient for them to run a carrier service between Stowmarket and Brettenham on Market days before the regular bus service was started. During

At Water Hall Farm, Brettenham circa 1911 parents Arthur & Emily Ayling-Turner with their children (l. to r.) Emily Ruth, Charles Edwin, Arthur George (seated), Frederick and Mary

Fasbourn Cottages, Buxhall with a Turner's van parked at the side

Arthur (Bruv) with his trade bike outside his wet fish shop in Stowupland Street

The first of the bungalows built by Arthur Ayling-Turner at Tot Hill in 1933

Family and friends gathered at the bungalow at Tot Hill

A general view of the Crown Street Premises

this period, Arthur had a wet fish shop in Stowupland Street called **McArthur's** and Emily Ruth had a wine shop in Station Road known as E. R. **Turner's**, which continued after her marriage to George **Pettitt**. By 1924 the family had moved again, this time to 29, Station Road (later to become Charlie **Codd's** bicycle shop) as well as premises further around the corner in Stowupland Street, which later became **Hopgood's** wallpaper department. The 1925 Kelly's directory has them listed as **Turner Bros.**, wholesale confectioners, 29 Station Road. However, they were only there for about two more years as by 1928 they had moved to 56 Crown Street. This soon became their established place of business and continued for the next forty-four years. They next appear in the 1933 Kelly's directory with the telephone number 148. At about this time Arthur, with the help of his son Arthur (Bruv), began building the first of a series of bungalows at Tot Hill close to where the garage site is. The first bungalow was occupied by George and Emily **Pettitt**, his daughter and son-in-law. By the time the 1937 Kelly's appeared the family business had become a Limited Company and was listed as **Turner** Bros (Stowmarket) Ltd. at the same address. Charles' daughter Jean remembers from her childhood that many of the customers were either running the village post-offices or the local public houses and she recalls often helping her father with the deliveries; at the pubs she would stop for her sandwiches and have a bottle of ginger beer (from bottles with a glass marble stopper in the neck). Jean states that many of the customers became like friends and that 'one elderly lady always gave me something when I called and I still have a china brooch that she gave me'.

(Above) Emily Ayling-Turner (née Divall). The van is advertising Smith's potato crisps on the side of the roof cage and Mackintosh's Carnival Assortment De-luxe sweets and toffees

(Left)Fred Ayling-Turner at the wheel with Arthur (Bruv) opening the door of the garage in Crown Street

During this period the Stowmarket shops supplied by **Turner** Bros were: **Meacham's** in Union Street; Regent Street had Mrs **Baker**, Mr **Garrard & Girlings**; Mr **Franklin** in Cardinals Road; Bury Street was Mr **Brett**, Mr **Ames** and 'Deafy' **Hill**; Charlie **Clarke's** in Bury Road; in Stowupland Road was Mr **Beaumont's**; and Creeting Road Corner was Mr **Oldfield**; the 'Tuppenny' Shop in Stowupland Street was supplied as well as Miss **Gooding**, Mrs **Seaman**, Mrs F **Ames** and **Proctor's**; Station Road had **Lillistone's**, Mr **Wright's** and **Pollard's**; Ipswich Street had Mr **Howard's**, Mr **Cunnold's** and the 'Bell' managed by Iris **Gosling**; Mrs **Scarf** in Childer Road; Messrs **Last** and **Cook** in Lime Tree Place; Messrs **Long**, **Brewster** and **Pleasance** at Combs Ford. The orders would be collected by somebody riding around the town on a bicycle on a Monday and deliveries would be made by Charles on a Tuesday morning. Further afield their van would supply towns such as Haverhill, Mildenhall, Long Melford, Sudbury, Hadleigh, Brandon, Ely, Soham, Littleport, Thetford, Diss, Bungay and Framlingham, plus all towns and villages in between. Their area bordered on, but did not include, Ipswich or towards the coast, as that area had its own suppliers. One of the early vans had a cage on the roof where were stored empty **Smith's** crisp tins (each tin had held two dozen packets) and returnable sweet jars on which there was a charge. In 1939 the brothers bought an 'International' van from **Barnard's**, but the Second World War quickly arrived and Arthur went to work at the Gasworks whilst Charles went to the Imperial Chemicals Industry (I.C.I.) for the duration of the war. Fred and Arthur senior carried on running the business, although rationing made it very difficult. During this period Fred was active in the Home Guard and was involved with radio message interception, for which he received a commendation. Afterwards Fred returned to the business and ran it single-handedly, whilst Charles eventually took over the Childer Road shop that was known by many as the 'tuck shop', as it was close to the schools in Violet Hill Road and Walnut Tree Walk.

Jean with her father Charles Ayling-Turner

(l. to r.) May, Fred and Arthur (Bruv) beside their van at the Crown Street premises

Ernie Durrant who helped with deliveries

The Crown Street premises with May arriving by bicycle and Mr Pleasance of Lime Tree Place with his trade bike at the warehouse door

Charles (left) and Alfred enjoying some refreshments beside their van. The roof cage for collecting the returned tins and sweet jars can be clearly seen

Many will remember the various company names associated with the confectionery business which provided the mainstay of **Turner's** trade such as, Blue Bird toffee, **Cadbury's** chocolate, **Sharp's** toffee, **Bassett's** Liquorice Allsorts, **Mackintosh's** chocolate, **Bassett's** Jelly babies, **Weston's** Wagon wheels, **Terry's** of York 'All Black' and Moonlight selections, **Fry's** chocolate (peppermint cream and Turkish Delight), **Payne's** Poppets, **Rowntree's** Aero and Kit Kat chocolate, fruit pastilles and gums, **Callard** and **Bowser's** butterscotch and toffee, **Caley's** chocolate, **Fox's** Glacier mints and fruits, **Trebor** mints, pear drops and sherbet lemons, Colonel **Walter's** 'Palm Toffee' and **Keiller** butterscotch. As well as traditional sweets and chocolates, old fashioned cough remedies such as Victory-V's and Fishermen's Friend etc were supplied. **Lyon's** fruit pies were delivered each week by train from London and brought to the Crown Street premises by a small three-wheeled articulated lorry.

Children of the period visiting the various shops would stare at the array of glass jars containing barley twist sticks and humbugs, toffee bon-bons and also hazelnut fondants etc. which were sold loose and bought in either 2oz or 4oz bags. Other items supplied by **Turner's** to tempt the children were sherbet dips, Jamboree Bags, penny lollies, drumstick lollies, fruit salads, black jacks, gob-stoppers and aniseed balls. In addition to these delights, **Turner's** also supplied **Jacob's** and **Frear's** biscuits, **Libby's, Heinz** and Epicure sweet and savoury tins and jars, plus large bags of peanuts in shells. The **Turner** children were only allowed to have minimal samples of some of the sweets and looked

A Turner's delivery van advertising Trebor's sweets

1593

TELEPHONE :
STOWMARKET 474

BTS

STATION :
STOWMARKET (EASTERN REGION)

56, CROWN STREET, BURY ROAD,
STOWMARKET,...

TURNER BROS. (STOWMARKET) LTD.

WHOLESALE CONFECTIONERS

TO..

forward to special events such as Easter, when they would get to share the broken Easter eggs. In the 1950's 'Dicky Bird' Christmas Crackers of London were supplied from **Turner's** to the children's ward at Anglesea Road hospital in Ipswich. These crackers were known to contain nice gifts and would bring some pleasure to the unfortunate children who had to stay in hospital over the Christmas period.

Fred married Edith **Scarff** in 1927 and had three daughters: Joy, Hazel and Jennifer. Charles married Violet **Leggett** and had Jean and Gillian; Emily Ruth married George **Pettitt** and adopted a son, Philip. The **Pettitts**, after leaving the wine shop in Station Road, took over the running of the Childer Road shop from Mrs **Scarff** before passing the business to Charles and Violet in 1951. Elizabeth married Joseph **Page** and had Susan and Robert. Arthur (Bruv), died April 1987 aged ninety-one, and May, who died January 1988 aged eighty-three, never married. Arthur senior died in June 1947 aged seventy-five and his wife Emily died March 1956. Hazel married Eric **Farrow** in 1956 and Jennifer married Adrian **Bridger** in 1960 and both these sons-in-law helped in the business, eventually taking over the running of the company when Fred retired in April 1969. Fred died two years later in February 1971 aged seventy-one. They continued until 1974 when marketing was changing radically with the introduction of the supermarkets and the decline of the small village and corner shops, making it unviable for such an enterprise to continue successfully. Charles died in February 1985 aged eighty-two, Elizabeth died in May 2000 aged eighty-six and Emily died at Hadleigh in Essex in 1984 aged eighty-six. ❑

TURNER BROS. (STOWMARKET) LTD.

WHOLESALE CONFECTIONERS
AND SUNDRYMEN

56 CROWN STREET, STOWMARKET

Representative
FRED AYLING TURNER

No. 3 TAVERN STREET
STOWMARKET

Turner & Co

GROCER & WINE MERCHANT

Charles **Turner** was baptised at Barnham in Suffolk on 1st December 1816, son of Thomas and Elizabeth (née **Chambers**). Charles later married a Miss Ellen **Fiske** of Chediston and lived for some while at Stoke Ferry in Norfolk, where they had at least seven children of which there were two sons, Charles and Louis and five daughters Jane, Ellen, Kate, Gertrude and Annie. By 1868, Charles senior had moved with his family to Stowmarket and set up in business in the Market Place, in a part of the building occupied by Joseph Antrim **Lankester**. **Lankester's** business was already well established and he traded as grocer and draper as well as a wine and spirit merchant. A commercial directory of Stowmarket dated 1868 shows Charles **Turner** & Co., grocer and draper, and also Eustace Frederick **Lankester**, importer of foreign wines and spirits, both trading in the Market Place. An 1873 directory has Charles **Turner** & Co. at Lankester House, Market Place alongside the business of Lankester & Wells, wine, spirit, ale & porter merchants. Charles bought the lease from Eustace F. **Lankester** in 1876. Gertrude, daughter of Charles and Ellen, died 19th April 1879 aged only nineteen.

The 1881 census lists Charles aged sixty-five, grocer and draper, born Barnham, Ellen aged fifty-one, born Chediston, and their daughters Jane aged twenty and Annie aged sixteen, both born in Stoke Ferry, Norfolk. Charles, son of Charles and Ellen, was working at this time as a fifteen-year-old grocer's assistant for a Mrs Emily **Colborne**, who had a grocer's and draper's shop in High Street, Hadleigh, Suffolk. Their eldest daughter, Ellen, was an eighteen-year-old governess for a Mr Walter **Collins** of Hunston. Their other son, Louis, who was aged twenty-four, does not appear in Suffolk at the time of the 1881 census. He may have worked at St Helier on the Channel Island of Jersey, as there is a Louis **Turner** aged twenty-four, grocer's shopman (birthplace simply given as England) lodging at 29, La Motte Street, St Helier with the **McDermott** family. On 6th May the following year Louis **Turner** (grocer), married Emmeline **Steggall**, daughter of John Redgen **Steggall** and Harriet (née **Coleby**), of Old Newton, at Wetherden church. By 1888 the business had become known as **Turner** & Co. and had taken on the wine and spirit trade although **Lankester** & **Wells** were still in business. They also arranged funerals, providing a hearse that was propelled by the bearers. Charles and Ellen had retired by the time of the 1891 census and were living at their home 'Danecroft', Finborough Road

Louis Turner

aged seventy-five and sixty-one respectively, along with their unmarried daughters Kate, thirty-five, Jane, twenty-nine and Ellen, twenty-eight. The 1891 census shows that Louis, aged thirty-five, a Master grocer, had taken over the running of the business. The census also lists Louis' wife, Emmeline, aged thirty-five with their children May aged six, Louis F. aged five, Hugh aged four, Russell aged three, Winifred aged two and Stanley aged one. (Alice Hilda, Louis and Emmeline's first child, died in 1885 aged two). Cyril, the eighth child was born in May, the month after the census was taken. The three-storey Market Place premises were also home to six other people, including three grocer's assistants namely, Albert **Rayner**, aged twenty-two from Saffron Walden, Essex; William **Sage** aged twenty-two from Tattingstone and William **Scott** aged sixteen from Felsham. The children's governess was Maud **Steggall** aged twenty-five from Old Newton (probably a relation of Emmeline);

Emmeline Turner (née Steggall)

Circa 1890, Charles Turner standing in the doorway of his shop with the Turner's hand-cart waiting to be loaded with produce for local delivery

the household also included domestic servants, Lucy **Smith** aged nineteen, cook and Elizabeth **Whitman** housemaid, both of Ipswich. In 1892 the competition between **Turner** & Co and **Lankester** & **Wells** was still the case, with **Lankester** & **Wells** proclaiming in their directory listing: (also at the "Drapery", Northampton) wine, spirit and cigar importers & bonders, ale & stout merchants & bottlers; Established 1785; offices & vaults, Market Place; bonded warehouse near railway station. Telegraphic address: **Lankester** Stowmarket. Specialities: - Proprietors of the celebrated "Oban" blend Scotch whisky & "Banshee" blend Irish whisky (both registered); also the high class brand of champagne "De La Roncière & Cie". Charles **Turner** died on 3rd April 1893 aged seventy-seven at his home 'Danecroft' Finborough Road and was buried in Stowmarket's Old Cemetery in Bury Road.

The business under Louis began to be altered to adjust to local competition by passing the drapery trade over to William **Turner** (Stowmarket) Ltd. (no relation) and concentrating on the grocery and wine and spirit trade. This ensured the continued use of the large vaults that had been well-known from when owned by **Lankester's**. The vaults were thought to be parts of a passageway that ran from Abbot's Hall under the Market Place to the church, the section that ran under the shop and part of the Market Place being bricked up and used as wine cellars. Emmeline used to make two large batches of bread every week and did all her own cooking; she also 'sweet pickled' hams, chaps and breast of bacon that used to hang in the kitchen as well as making her own mincemeat at Christmas. Louis and Mr Bromley **Saunders**, an auctioneer for **Hunt**, **Peddar** & **Knight**, were the first joint Honorary Secretaries of the Old Bathing Place, situated in a section of the Rattlesden river beside **Boulter's** Mill, when it was first opened in 1888.

The children of Louis and Emmeline were educated at the **Theobold's** Grammar school in Needham Market (currently **Lloyd's** Bank and **Gudgeon** & **Prentice** solicitors). After leaving school, brothers Louis Frank (known as Frank) and Hugh joined the family business, helping their parents in the shop until the outbreak of the First World War. An extract from the hand-written memoirs of Hugh states that "In 1914, I joined the Navy and went to sea for three and half years as a Seaman Gunner". In 1916, Ellen, an unmarried daughter of Charles and Ellen, died aged fifty-three. After the War, Frank and Hugh continued working in the shop alongside their parents until the death of their father, Louis, on 9th December 1922 aged sixty-six. Louis' mother, Ellen, had by this time moved to Ipswich, where she died on Valentine's Day 14th February 1926 aged ninety-eight. The business continued to be managed by Frank and Hugh until the untimely death on 19th May 1934 of Frank aged only forty-nine. The obituary of Louis Frank **Turner** lists many of the clubs and societies he was actively involved with, including the British Legion, the Rookery Bowls Club and an early member of the local tennis club. He was also a member of the Chamber of Trade and an attendant at the Parish church, but it gives his main hobby as gardening. The mourners at his funeral service consisted of virtually all the prominent businessmen and dignitaries in the town at that time.

On 7th October 1933, at Stowmarket Parish Church, Hugh, aged forty-seven, married Miss Gwendolen Emily **Lucas**, aged twenty-three, daughter of the late Herbert Frank **Lucas** and Emily Ann (née **Perring**) from Spelbrook near Bishops Stortford. (Herbert **Lucas** had died on 11th February 1912 aged only twenty-eight.) When Gwendolen was fourteen in 1924, her mother and second husband, Charles **Palmer**, whom she had married in 1915, moved to Finborough Road, Stowmarket, where he took up the post of music and English teacher at the Grammar School in Violet Hill Road. Gwendolen, who was born 1st January 1910, had a younger sister, Mavis, whom she helped to look after as a child. After their marriage, Hugh and Gwendolen lived above Norman **Ward's** shoe shop on the opposite side of the road. Gwendolen remembers the austere time during the Second World War when everything was on ration and due to the fact that the young men who had previously helped in the shop had gone into the services, she had to go around the town getting orders. Frank looked after the accounts and Winifred looked after the house etc. Hugh was helped in the shop by Mr Ernest **Durrant** and Mr Len **Elsey**. Ernest had joined the business as a young man aged fourteen and a half in 1928 serving a three year apprenticeship as a grocer and provisions assistant. Len joined the company from Woodbridge in 1930, as a full assistant. Ernest remembers that most grocery items, such as sugar and tea, as well as herbs and spices, were bought loose in bulk. Sugar had to be weighed and packed in blue bags and commodities such as dried fruit etc. were flat wrapped and tucked, as were butter, margarine and lard. Customers were able to sample the cheeses on request: a core sample was taken and a cracker biscuit provided for people to try. Ernest believes that many people probably took advantage of this to enjoy a free snack when they felt peckish. He also remembers that one counter was solely for wines and spirits. Wine was sold in full, half and quarter bottles; ports and sherries were available, as well as six different brands of whisky. A trade bike was used to deliver groceries to the people in the town and a half-ton Ford van (registration

(left) Hugh Turner and (right) Winifred Turner

Turner's shop front decorated up to mark the visit to the town of the County Agricultural Show in July 1913

Gwendolen Turner (née Lucas) dressed as the Golly on the Duke's Head meadow circa 1924 (Ipswich Street houses in background)

The wedding photograph of Hugh Turner and Gwendolen Emily Lucas in the grounds behind their premises in the Market Place October 7th 1933

number RT 8467) was used for the surrounding villages; it was in this van that Ernest learnt to drive. The desire of shopkeepers to please in those days was paramount. Ernest remembers one occasion when a customer, who had omitted one item from his order, requested by telephone that the item, one lemon costing 1½d, be delivered promptly to a large house in the town. Ernest was given the task, but unfortunately delivered the lemon to the front door in error, receiving a sharp rebuke for not delivering to the backdoor that was reserved for tradesmen. In 1937 he left to take a manager's post in London which he held until the outbreak of war. In 1945 Ernest returned to work for **Turner** & Co in Stowmarket, staying for another five years.

Emmeline **Turner**, widow of Louis, died at 28, Market Place 21st October 1944, aged eighty-seven. Gwendolen remembers serving tea and coffee to soldiers billeted in the Drill Hall in Finborough Road and one night even allowed three of the servicemen the luxury of a hot bath at her home. After the War the business continued trading in the town for another eight years and many people might remember buying "**Turner's**" broken biscuits, their own cuts of cheese or bacon and the smell of their fresh ground coffee. Hugh was President of the Ipswich and District Grocers' Association. Away from the business, Hugh and Gwendolen also involved themselves within the local community: Hugh was District Scout Master, being involved with many Gang Shows and was also a Lay Reader at the Parish Church, continuing the latter until he was eighty-two. Gwendolen was also involved with the Scouting movement as a Cub mistress and was a Mothers' Union member at the Parish Church. They were both Sunday School teachers there.

The shop opening hours were the same as most other shops in the town, opening at 8:00am and staying open until 6:00pm closing from 1:00 till 2:00pm for lunch with

Another view of Turner's shop.
The two shop workers are probably Ernest Durrant (left) and Sidney Hammond

Ernest off to collect orders as he did every Monday, Wednesday and Friday morning

early closing on Tuesdays. On Thursday market days during the winter months, times were a bit more flexible, as Hugh was very often late for his lunch because he would stay behind in the shop to enable one or two customers to shelter in relative comfort while waiting for the bus. The employees were entitled to two weeks' holiday per year. Cups of tea, made in the kitchen of the house, were provided for the shop staff at break times, being brought in on a tray by a maid. The breaks were taken in a covered alley with bench seats at the side of the shop. At Christmas time, as well as being given a Christmas box, the staff were treated to a free Christmas Supper that was usually held on the 23rd in the breakfast room. **Turner** & Co were also known for their charity at Christmas by providing food parcels for some of the poorer people in the town.

The business and premises were bought by the F. W. **Woolworth** chain on 1st August 1953. Hugh and Gwendolen retired and moved to Chelsea Close, Ipswich in

Turner's delivery van, registration number RT 8467, in which Ernest Durrant learned to drive

Some of Turner's shop staff
top (l. to r.) Bill Garrod, Maurice Wilding, Sidney Hammond and Fred Wilding
above (l. to r.) Sidney Hammond, Ernest Durrant and Bill Garrod

1954. Hugh **Turner** died 19th May 1977 aged ninety years. A dog-eared but treasured possession kept by Gwendolen is a "Special Pass" for the bearer and friend to view "Quest" and show attention, signed by E. H. **Shackleton**, which had been presented to Hugh. The "Quest" was the boat on which the explorer Sir Ernest Henry **Shackleton** died of heart failure following a bout of influenza on 5th January 1921 while heading for Antarctica; his body was buried on the island of South Georgia.

The shop front changed very little following the changeover and many people who went into the early 'Woolies' will remember the glass bowled lamps that hung throughout

Hugh Turner

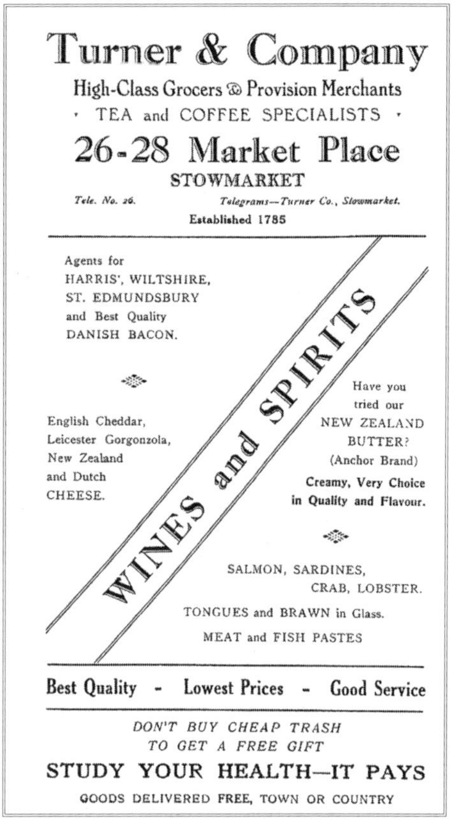

the shop. Eventually, however, the old building was demolished to make way for a larger store, but an interesting note from the memoirs of Hugh **Turner** describes the old building as consisting of "a large fourteen room house, three storey warehouse, large vaults and was originally the Old White Hart Inn. The inside of the shop was once "the covered in" way for the coach and horses and some of the stables still stand". This must not be confused with the White Hart which used to be in Crowe Street, currently **Lacy Scott** & **Knight**'s, an inn from before 1830 until the 1960's. ❑

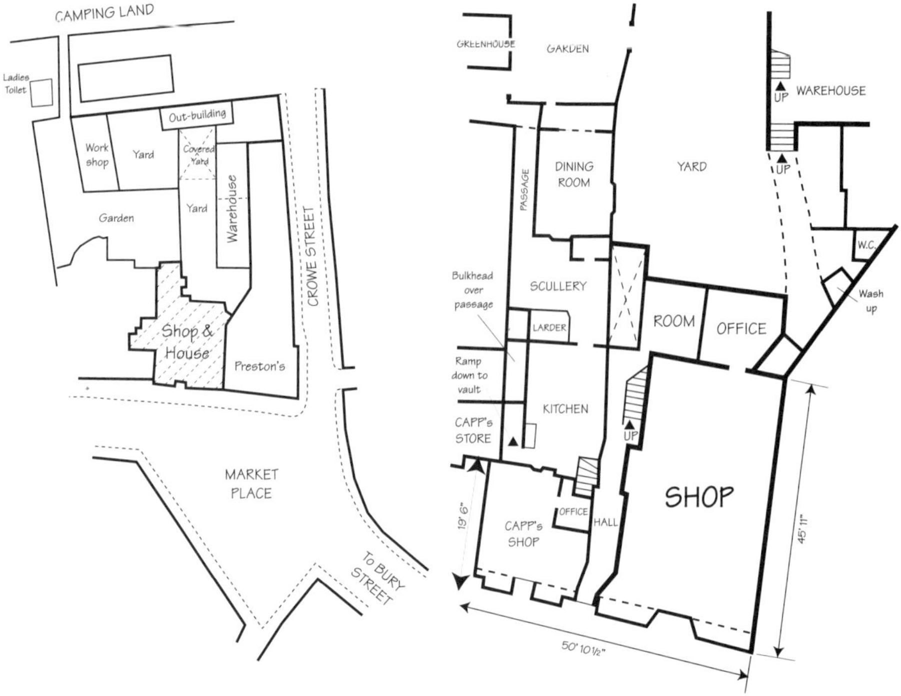

A plan (l.) showing the location of Turner's shop and (r.) detail of the layout drawn from information supplied by Gwendolen Turner

The shop just prior to its closure in 1952 (taken by Gwendolen Turner)

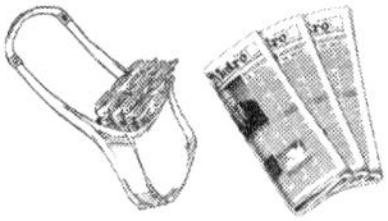

Webb's

SUNDAY NEWSPAPER DISTRIBUTORS

Many people will remember the row of Victorian terraced cottages next to the "Durdans" in Bury Street which was demolished in the early 1990's to make way for the roundabout at the start of the 'Inner Relief Road' at the junction with Crown Street and Violet Hill. Some older people may also remember a large blue enamelled sign advertising 'The News of the World' fixed on the wall of the end cottage (see photograph below). This was from where Arthur **Barnard** (also known as **Webb**) started Stowmarket's first wholesale delivery of Sunday newspapers in the early 1890's, the News of the World being the first of many different names over the years.

The 1881 census lists Arthur **Barnard**, aged thirty, living at Bury Street with his trade given as gardener/journeyman, born Stowmarket. His wife was Eliza (née **Scruby**) aged 27, with sons Ernest, aged six, Herbert, aged three and daughter Ada, aged one, all born at Stowmarket. Percy, another son, was born later that year on 5th December and his surname was registered as **Webb**. The 1891 census lists the family all as **Barnards** with: Arthur, forty-two, a grocer/gardener; Eliza, thirty-nine, his wife; Ernest, sixteen, son, maltster's labourer; Herbert, thirteen, son, leather factory hand; Ada, eleven, daughter, Percy, nine, son and Alice, seven, daughter, all scholars born at Stowmarket. Throughout his school years, Percy was known by his **Webb** surname and later, as a young teenager, he would help his father collect the newspapers, with a handcart, from the station.

Percy **Webb** married Violet Gertrude (Gert) **Cook** of Trimley, daughter of Henry **Cook**, railway plate layer, in 1903 at Stowmarket Methodist Chapel. Their first child, Beatrice Nellie Violet **Webb**, was born in 1904 at Ham Row, Stowmarket and their son,

Bury Street, showing the end terrace cottage where Arthur Barnard established a Sunday newspaper delivery business in the early 1890's. A 'New of the World' sign is just visible on the wall

Charles Henry (Charlie) **Webb**, was born in 1905 at Bury Street. By 1916 the family lived at 24, Regent Street and during the week Percy worked at **Thurlow's** leather belting works in Bury Street and also as a gardener at Temple Bar for the **Thurlow** family. Early on Sunday mornings, Percy and Gert would push their handcart to the railway station to collect the newspapers from the London train, taking them home to sort in their front room. As well as people calling at the house to buy their Sunday papers, Percy was the first Sunday paper man to deliver in Stowmarket, as he was the sole agency holder in the town. After attending local schools, Charlie left at the age of thirteen and worked with his father, both gardening and at the leather belting works. He later became a crane driver at the Suffolk Iron Foundry in Prentice Road.

Arthur Barnard Webb

It was at the marriage of his sister, Beatrice to Thomas Stanley (Tom) **Alexander** from Cotton, on 22nd January 1927 at Stowmarket Parish Church, that Charlie met his bride-to-be, Agnes Louisa (Topsy) **Baker**, born 4th November 1908 at Westhorpe. Topsy had attended the village school at Finningham until she was fourteen years old; she then became apprentice to the village dressmaker for a year. She later found employment as a sewing-maid at Stow Lodge Hospital, working on a daily basis and lodging with an aunt in Regent Street, Stowmarket. Charlie courted Topsy for two years and they married in 1929 at Eye Register Office. Charlie and Topsy had two children, Sheila Jean (Jean) born 1930 and Owen Charles (Bob), born October 1932 at 78, Union Street, Stowmarket. During the 1930's, Charlie carried on working at the foundry and helping his father with the Sunday paper rounds while Topsy raised her young family. The Kelly's directory for 1937 lists P. **Webb** and Son, Newsagents at 24, Regent Street. During the War years Charlie stayed at the foundry, as it was a reserved occupation; he also served as a Column Officer in the National Fire Service based in Union Street until his discharge on 19th April 1945. In 1944, Percy gave up the rounds, passing the business over to Charlie and Topsy. Charlie then finished working at the foundry. Their children, Jean and Bob, helped with the rounds for a few years until they left school and went to college and university. Topsy used to deliver papers between the railway gates in Stowupland Road to the 'Black Barn', Stowupland. The rounds continued to be built up until they had seventeen boys on the books delivering to the villages as far out as Earl Stonham, Mendlesham Green, Old Newton, Haughley, Earls Green, Harleston, Onehouse, Buxhall and Finborough. At 3:30 in the morning they would get up and go by car to a railway wagon that had been left in a siding at Stowmarket railway station. From

Charlie Webb in his National Fire Service uniform

here the nine thousand newspapers were collected in two trailer loads and taken to a hired shop in Stowupland Street, formerly belonging to Charlie **Mills**, shoemaker. Some of the Sunday newspapers of that time, The News of the World, The Times, The Observer and The Express are still published today, but there were many others: The Sunday Graphic, The Empire News, The **Reynold's** News, The Sunday Dispatch, The Sunday Pictorial and The Sunday Chronicle, all now disappeared from circulation. Then in the 1950's the business was transferred to some garages in Bury Street, behind Vic **Norman's** fish shop, that Charlie had paid £37 for in 1937, originally Town Charity Land. Topsy well remembers sitting on her own in the Bury Street property at 4:30 am inserting supplements into the relevant newspapers. This mammoth task had to be completed by 7:00am when some of the delivery boys called to collect their quota of newspapers for the day. It was Topsy's specific job to "get the boys out and get the boys in." Charlie would deliver the batches of newspapers to the roundsmen who lived in the outlying villages and afterwards take a selection of newspapers to Stow Lodge Hospital as well as to The Creamery in Cemetery Lane (Violet Hill Road). This used to take him most of the morning as so many of his customers wanted to stop and chat to him. One of the roundsmen was William Douglas (Bill) **Williams** who lived in Valley View Road and delivered to all of Combs. Bill's son, David, took on one part of the round as a paperboy in the mid 1950's and covered Poplar Hill, The Crescent and Hillside, receiving eight shillings 8/- (40p) per week. David remembers the papers being delivered to their house and sorted in the front room. The round took three hours from 8:00am till 11:00am and included

Charlie with daughter Sheila Jean outside their house in Regent Street

Webb's premises, 24 Regent Street

practically every house in those streets. The money was also collected at this time (including one penny for delivery) and was often trustingly left on the windowsill or step. Some families had two or even three papers Once the boys were back, Topsy would return home to cook Sunday lunch for the family. The afternoon would be spent counting out the day's takings on the kitchen table. The money would be methodically piled with notes and coins in descending value to facilitate the banking procedure. The price of the papers during this period was 2d (less than 1p) for the News of the World and 3d (just over 1p) for the Times; there was no delivery charge to begin with, but later ½d had to be added to cover costs. All of the newspapers had 'local representatives' who used to call on Topsy and Charlie at regular intervals to discuss the circulation figures and special promotions in their respective newspapers.

Charlie Webb

In the late 1940's and early 1950's, Charlie and Topsy's other interests centred around their racing greyhounds, which they entered for competitions at the Ipswich, Bury St Edmunds and Norwich tracks. Charlie and Topsy were also keen card players and for a number of years both played in the local cribbage league. Topsy also became one of the founder members of the Royal British Legion (Women's Section) in Stowmarket. They moved from Regent Street to **Gowle** Road in 1953; the business carried on at the site of the old stables where extra revenue was brought in due to the fact that Bury Street was part of the

Agnes Louisa (Topsy) and Charlie Webb

A45 trunk road and passing trade was brisk. This invariably caused occasional traffic problems.

The business continued until 1972 when Charlie and Topsy sold the Bury Street property and rounds to Mr Trevor **Meggs** (agencies cannot be passed on or sold) who carried on for over sixteen years until August 1988, when it was then passed on to Mr and Mrs Dennis (Denny) **Fryett**. Charlie **Webb** died 21st May 1982 aged seventy-seven. On 7th September 1997 the business was sold to Mr Frederick and Mrs Olwin **Sayer** at J & S Stores (formerly known as The Creamery) in Bury Street.

Topsy died in June 2004 in her ninety-sixth year. She maintained a keen sense of humour and enjoyed visits from a large contingent of friends and acquaintances accumulated over many years. She also derived a great deal of pleasure from listening to literary audio tapes and admitted that her favourite was the poetry of John **Betjeman**, much of which she knew by heart.

In August 1999, the round was taken over by Stuart and Chrissy **Basten** of Creeting Stores, Creeting Road. This is the first time that the Sunday round has been run by newsagents offering a full seven-day service and therefore no longer really exists as a completely separate entity. ❑

The former shoemaker's shop in Stowupland Street, hired by the Webbs as a distribution centre for their Sunday newspaper businesss prior to using premises in Bury Street (below)

The garages behind Norman's Fish and Chip shop in Bury Street from where Webb's Sunday newspapers were distributed from the late 1950's

TANNERS

Webb and Son (Combs)Ltd

The first known recorded business of tanning leather appeared at Combs in 1710 when Thomas **Denny** was given £100 by his father, also Thomas, to 'sink' a Tanyard. The sinking referred to the digging of a series of pits which were where many of the various parts of the process took place. The pits were usually between six and eight feet deep and filled with an assortment of liquids and chemicals depending on each phase of the operation. The initial stage was when the hides were soaked for the first two weeks of the process, which loosened the hair. This tanyard was set up next to **Denny's** Farm in what is now Tannery Road, Combs, a house that had been occupied by the same family since the fifteenth century. It was run by Thomas and his son, also Thomas, for several years. Thomas (II) retired in 1748 (died 1772) and the business passed to Thomas (III). However, prior to Thomas's (II) retirement, he had employed a young man from County Antrim in Ireland whose name was Joseph Antrim **Webb**. When Thomas (III) retired in 1776 (died 1803), Joseph, who was employed as a manager, was in a position to buy the house which is now part of the Tannery Office complex and also lease the Tanyard from the **Denny** family, most of whom had emigrated to America.

Joseph Antrim's son, also Joseph Antrim (born 1777), soon joined the business at a young age and together formed the partnership of **Webb** & Son. Joseph (I) retired from the business in 1809 and died the same year aged sixty-nine. The following year Joseph (II) and his wife Elizabeth (née **Lankester**) had a son who they also named Joseph Antrim (III), who was to become a partner in the business at the age of twenty-two, but who unfortunately died the following year in 1833. Joseph (II) then continued the dynasty by offering the partnership to his second son, Lankester (born 1812). With these two men at the helm, still trading as **Webb** and Son, Combs Tannery entered a time of great prosperity, taking full advantage of the growth of industry in the nineteenth century with its attendant demand for all manufactured products. Joseph (II) retired in 1848, moving from Combs to live at The Hollies, a substantial house on the site of today's Post Office Sorting Office in Ipswich Street, leaving Lankester to conduct the business on his own. The 1844 edition of White's Directory of Suffolk lists in the Combs parish '**Webb** Jph. A. & Son, tanners, curriers, fellmongers, manure manufacturers, wool staplers etc., Combs Tannery, and Stowmarket.' Alongside that entry is '**Webb** Lankester, corn and coal merchant, maltster, etc., Tannery'. The text from the same page also states that 'here is a large Tannery etc. belonging to J. A. **Webb** and Son., who employ 100 hands, and during the last two years have been boring an artesian well, and have now got to the depth of 900 feet without finding soft water for which they are searching. The bore is ten inches in diameter at the surface, and many interesting geological specimens have been extracted.' The well had to be bored another eighty feet before reaching water. Joseph Antrim (II) died February 1864 aged eighty-six.

Lankester **Webb** married Sarah **Vertue**, who was a member of a banking family from Woodbridge and had eight children, four boys and four girls. However, the 1851 census index lists Joseph Antrim **Webb** (II) as being aged seventy-three, born Combs, with wife Elizabeth age sixty-six born London and daughter Louisa age thirty-one born Combs, all living at Stowmarket and Lankester **Webb** aged thirty-eight born Combs with wife Sarah the same age, born Woodbridge and children: Anne (Annie) age six, Lucy aged four, Octavius aged 2 and Catherine aged six months. Where Sarah Pitcairn **Webb**, their oldest child born 1837, Joseph Vertue **Webb**, who would have been aged thirteen and the other two sons, Edward born 1840 and Walter born 1841, were at the time of the census is not known. Three of Lankester's sons died unmarried before reaching the age of twenty-five: Edward Lankester died February 1863 aged twenty two, Octavius died October 1866 aged eighteen, only a few months after his mother, Sarah, who had died in the July aged fifty-three. Walter Byles died April 1867 aged twenty-five. This left Joseph Vertue, who went into the business, but also never married and made it appear that the link would be broken.

Lankester Webb with his wife Sarah (née Vertue) surrounded by seven of their eight children (youngest daughter Catherine had died aged two in 1852) Joseph Vertue Webb is standing, in the light jacket. Annie is standing at the back right of the picture, behind her unfortunate brothers Edward and Walter and beside Octavius. (photograph taken in Combs prior to 1863 when Edward, seated next to his mother, died)

The dynasty was maintained, however, by the fact that Lankester's daughter, Annie married George Robert **Portway** of Bury St. Edmunds in 1866 and subsequently moved to Leeds in Yorkshire; they had eight children: George Webb born 1867, Joseph Herbert born 1868, Annie Charlotte born 1869, Winifred Mary born 1872, Bertha Grace born 1876, Robert Benton born 1877, Ruth and Harold. Their eldest son, George Webb **Portway**, moved back to Combs in 1884 to go into business with his uncle, Joseph Vertue. George Webb **Portway** married Constance Maud **Ledger** in 1902 and had two children: George Ronald Webb **Portway** born 1904 and Constance Barbara (Barbara) born 1908. Barbara married Francis Whitehead **Gascoyne** and they eventually became known as the owners of Model Farm.

George Robert Portway and his wife Annie (née Webb) with George Webb Portway standing behind his mother (photograph taken in Leeds, Yorkshire)

During Lankester's time at the helm, the Tannery's fortunes soared, enabling him to buy farms and cottages as they came up for sale in the Combs area. These were used to house the growing number of employees at the Tannery and the fields were used to place their cattle and horses etc. as a part of their normal farming practice (the cow hides generally not used at the Tannery). This growth put them in the position of being "traders who ran a manufacturing company." Producing their own stock on their own farms was only part of the process, as from 1832 they also had to import hides, skins and part-tanned leather from all round the world, which were brought up the Stowmarket

Joseph Vertue Webb photographed at Combs by Arthur Bugg of Stowmarket

Navigation to Stowmarket. In 1865, Lankester realised an ambition by building his 'Model' Farm. Three sets of drawings were submitted for an architectural competition and the chosen design is still in existence today. The farming business, which was run concurrently with the Tannery, included the breeding of Suffolk horses and at its peak boasted fourteen fully brassed teams of these fine animals.

Leather tanning and curing was quite a lengthy and complicated procedure. In the eighteenth century it was quite common for the villagers to bring various small animal skins such as rabbit, hare, fox and badger to the Tannery for curing; later the next century it was mainly cow hides and sheepskins. The animals were slaughtered as early in the morning as possible, in order for the hides and skins to be dealt with within twenty-four hours. Other methods used by Eskimos and Kalahari bushmen were to chew it to make it supple, but so far there is no evidence to support this process in Combs!

Large quantities of oak bark were used for the tanning process due to the fact that that particular bark produces tannin (tannic acid) which seeps very slowly through the pores of the hide and drives out the water, tanning the fibres. How this process was discovered by early man remains a mystery! Huge quantities of this bark needed to be cut and stored at the Tannery; it was piled in vast stacks in the yard, resulting in employment for many local people which by the 1880's had reached

Combs Tannery circa 1864 showing the Carriage House and Curriers building

The Manager's House, Model Farm, Combs

nearly three hundred people. The continuing process of tanning involved the hides being lifted from the lime pits and washed. The hides were then draped over the fleshing beams where the excess fat and flesh was removed with fleshing knives. It was after this that the 'liquor' from the oak bark was used to tan the hides, a process which took three months, where the hides were continually moved from one pit of the solution into freshly steeped bark liquor. Following this the hides could spend anything between two months to two years 'laid away', depending on the type of process and finish required and then hung up to drip before being rolled dry. As many as two hundred and forty pits were being used for the different stages in the tanning process at the height of the Tannery's success. Most pits were full of the tannin liquid, level with the narrow walkways that separated them and on which the men had to walk to lift the poles draped with hides. It thus became a familiar sound to hear a splash when a person accidentally fell in; it was said that a man could not become a good tanner until he had been 'baptised' in the pits. Many of the men would wear locally made hand crafted wooden soled shoes with leather uppers which gave them better grip on the often slippery floors thoughout the factory. The knives, scrapers, fleshers and other tools essential for the trade would usually be made by a local blacksmith until more standardised tools became more the norm towards the end of the nineteenth century, when pamphlets appeared advertising 'patented' tools, being mass produced, which claimed to have improved cutting edges etc. Sole leather for the shoe and boot trade was produced as well as industrial belts for such as **Thurlow's** belting works in Stowmarket and used to drive the machinery in many factories and farm machinery powered by traction engines. They also produced the suction and delivery hoses for the local fire engines as well as leather buckets, straps and harnesses etc.

George Webb **Portway** introduced his son George Ronald Webb **Portway** into the business in 1925 at the age of twenty-one and after George Webb's death in 1943 George R. W., who had married Hebe **Cox**, took over the business and it was during this period that further changes were to take place, especially in the late 1950's when the heavy

Webb and Son's impressive business stationery

leather trade was feeling increasing competition from synthetic materials. The decision was made to concentrate solely on producing wooled sheepskins. The tannery then began producing Shearlings in large quantities for the shoe-lining, glove and clothing trades. This leather was produced from sheepskins from all over the world and sixty per cent of the articles made from this leather were then exported back to some of the countries of their origin. George and Hebe had a son Nicolas Webb (Nic) **Portway** in 1941 who joined the family firm in 1962 and worked alongside his father. Nic married Susan **Marshman** and had son James and daughter Rosalind.

The sheepskin process consisted of the raw material arriving from the abattoirs with some form of temporary preservation such as drying, salting or pickling etc. It was then soaked, trimmed, washed, fleshed and prepared for tanning. The wool may have been shorn at this point. The skin would then be pickled and tanned in a chromium solution obtained from mineral sources (superseding the bark process) after which the skin became leather. The tanned leather was washed to remove excess tanning materials and dried. De-greasing then took place to remove the large quantities of grease which were unevenly distributed over a sheepskin. The leather was then dried again, stretched out on a toggle frame to obtain a flat piece of leather of the greatest possible area, with an even surface for the subsequent processing. It was dampened down to obtain the correct

Circa 1905. Workers photographed with a selection of products produced by the tannery which included leather machine belts and leather fire buckets

moisture content condition for the next process, staking. This was the working of the leather to and fro to soften it. Staking was so named because the leather used to be softened by working it over a stake set in the ground; later sophisticated machines were used. For the next part of the process the leather was buffed on an abrasive wheel to produce a fine suede surface on the flesh side. After this the leather was sorted for dying, which was usually done in a drum or paddle. The skins were then retoggled, conditioned and restaked to restore the suede surface. Finally the wool was combed, shorn to length and ironed to give it a glossy lustre. This completed the manufacturing process; they were then sorted into qualities, measured, packed and despatched.

Since the end of the Second World War, changes in legislation and other factors, such as environmental concerns and health and safety rulings, led to consolidation of the industry and the ultimate demise of small localised tanneries. Whereas at that time there were three thousand five hundred tanneries, there are now less than forty; however, the Combs Tannery was able to keep production moving until 1988. George Ronald Webb **Portway** died in 1996, by which time Nic had already begun to bring diversity to the site by leasing the buildings to allow other businesses to set up various unit factories such as a joinery workshop, warehousing and packaging, accountancy, courier and distribution services, an asbestos advisory centre and an environmental engineer. This trend continues to be developed into the twenty-first century. Although there has been a change in the basic core business in the last fifteen years, with Nic as Managing Director and his son James as a director, this makes nearly two hundred years with nine generations of the family's connection with the Combs Tannery site. ❑

POEM

ABERY'S for home-cooked ham, French snails and foreign cheeses
BURROWS for potatoes, fresh fuit and veg that pleases

COOPER'S ran the buses, brought country folk to town,
DAY'S mens' shaves and ladies' perms would never let you down

DURRANT'S for your 'daily rag' and fountain pen repair
INCE'S for mens' working clothes, a barber for their hair

LAWSON'S ladies' underwear, big knickers and warm vest
MAYCOCK'S 'Galleon' coffee bar where drivers had a rest

MAYHEW'S for your fancies, fresh bread and wedding cake
MOSESSON that's Stramit, straw housing boards did make

NUNN'S for hand-made boots and shoes, fine quality, long wear
PIKE'S sold petrol at their pumps, did welding and repair

PROCTOR'S at the corner shop sold sweets and lemonade
RAY'S known for their coffee smells and tea in packets weighed

REVETT'S mopeds, motorbikes, three-wheelers and Lambretta
STEARN'S cosmetics, powders, creams and pills to make you better!

TIBBENHAM'S the Foundry made mowers for your grass
TURNER BROS wholesalers sold sweets and chocs first-class

TURNER'S in the Market Place, tinned food and deep wine cellars
WEBB'S for Sunday papers and all of them best-sellers

WEBB'S Tannery for sheepskin gloves and hats it then appears -
THESE TOO have been here faithfully,
TO SERVE YOU THROUGH THE YEARS.

sjc
June 2004

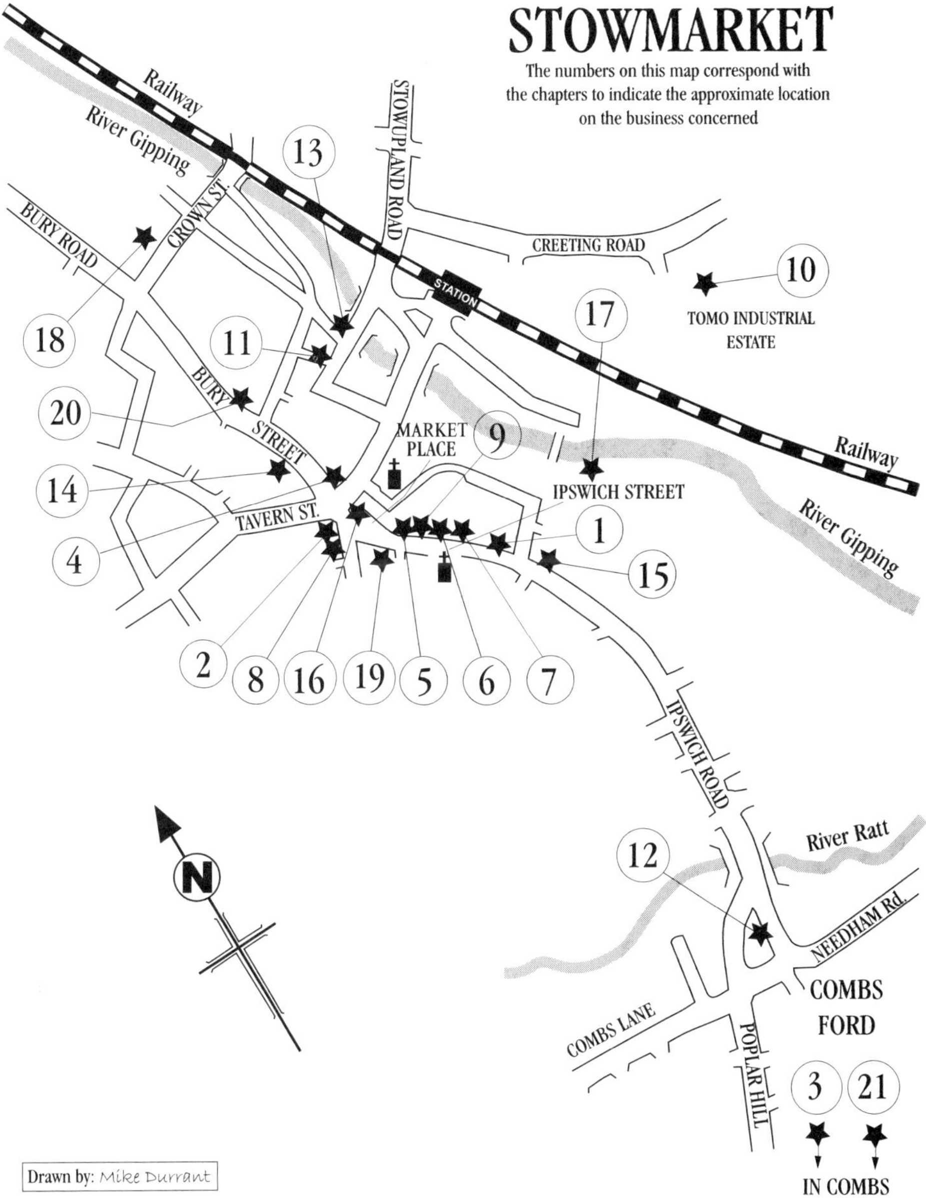
STOWMARKET
The numbers on this map correspond with
the chapters to indicate the approximate location
on the business concerned
Railway
River Gipping
BURY ROAD
CROWN ST.
STOWUPLAND ROAD
CREETING ROAD
STATION
TOMO INDUSTRIAL
ESTATE
BURY
STREET
MARKET
PLACE
TAVERN ST.
IPSWICH STREET
IPSWICH ROAD
River Ratt
NEEDHAM Rd.
COMBS
FORD
COMBS LANE
POPLAR HILL
IN COMBS
N
13
10
17
18
11
20
9
14
1
4
15
2
8
16
19
5
6
7
12
3
21
Drawn by: Mike Durrant

PRE-DECIMAL COINAGE

Most of the references to money in this book refer to the coinage which existed prior to the 15th February 1971 when the country officially changed over to a decimal currency system. A set of the coinage and notes in circulation prior to then are reproduced below. (The smallest coin, a farthing (¼d) (not shown), was withdrawn from circulation in 1960).

One pound note - £1

Ten Shilling note - 10/- (50p)

NICKEL BRASS

Threepence - 3d (1½p)

BRONZE

Penny - 1d

Halfpenny - 1/2d

CUPROL NICKEL

Halfcrown - 2/6d (12½p)

Florin 2/- (10p)

Shilling - 1/- (5p)

Sixpence - 6d (2½p)

INDEX

This simple keyword index, arranged alphabetically, lists selected names, places and events etc., from the text. *(Surnames are in bold type. Street names and places refer to Stowmarket unless otherwise stated)*

C

N

O

P

T

U

V